herstories

Rochelle Brock and Richard Greggory Johnson III
Executive Editors

Vol. 10

The Black Studies & Critical Thinking series
is part of the Peter Lang Education list.
Every volume is peer reviewed and meets
the highest quality standards for content and production.

PETER LANG
New York • Washington, D.C./Baltimore • Bern
Frankfurt • Berlin • Brussels • Vienna • Oxford

Judy A. Alston & Patrice A. McClellan

herstories

Leading with the Lessons of the Lives of Black Women Activists

PETER LANG
New York • Washington, D.C./Baltimore • Bern
Frankfurt • Berlin • Brussels • Vienna • Oxford

Library of Congress Cataloging-in-Publication Data
Alston, Judy A.
Herstories: leading with the lessons of the lives of Black women
activists / Judy A. Alston, Patrice A. McClellan.
p. cm. — (Black studies and critical thinking; v. 10)
Includes bibliographical references and index.
1. African American women—Biography. 2. African American leadership.
3. African American women civil rights workers—Biography.
4. African American women—Political activity—History.
I. McClellan, Patrice A. II. Title. III. Series.
E185.96.A564   323.092'396073—dc22   2011010653
ISBN 978-1-4331-1193-8 (hardcover)
ISBN 978-1-4331-1192-1 (paperback)
ISSN 1947-5985

Bibliographic information published by **Die Deutsche Nationalbibliothek**.
Die Deutsche Nationalbibliothek lists this publication in the "Deutsche
Nationalbibliografie"; detailed bibliographic data is available
on the Internet at http://dnb.d-nb.de/.

The paper in this book meets the guidelines for permanence and durability
of the Committee on Production Guidelines for Book Longevity
of the Council of Library Resources.

This book is dedicated to the voices of all Black women activists, those known and those unknown, upon whose shoulders we stand.

Judy: As always to my parents, George and Naomi Alston for their love and support; to my Godmother, Mrs. Anna Mae Bonaparte, one of those unknown Black women educator/activists from Charleston, SC; and to my life partner, Dr. Cynthia A. Tyson, who lovingly serves as my everyday inspiration and reality check.

Patrice: To my grandmother, Noleda Glover for always showing me unconditional love. I miss you; to my mother, Brenda Pettus for interceding on my behalf, words of wisdom, encouragement, and tough love; to my mentors Drs. Judy A. Alston and Cynthia A. Tyson for their high expectations, love, instruction, and support; and to my daughter Cassidy who is my inspiration and biggest fan. Mommy loves you.

Contents

Preface

The genesis of this book began in my first teaching position at the University of Houston (UH) in 1996. As a newly minted Ph.D. from The Pennsylvania State University (and the 5th ranked Educational Administration program in the country), I was once again in front of a group of students as the "teacher." (Just as an aside, I never had in my mind to enter the field of education until my mother gave me the "you need to have a teaching certificate to fall back on" speech in 1984 at the beginning of my sophomore at Winthrop College. Needless to say, she was and still is right and it's been almost 25 years of being an educator.) Here I was 31 years old with students who ranged in age from 20 to 50, and my previous teaching experience was with high school English students in my home state of South Carolina at Cainhoy High School and Brookland-Cayce High School. This was a new experience and a new chapter in my life-teaching Educational Leadership, Organizational Behavior, and Multicultural Issues in Education; I had undergraduates, masters, and doctoral students in my three years at UH. (Additionally I worked with high school students in a summer program, and I taught students at Houston Community College.) My teaching assignments led to the development of a research agenda that is still alive and well now some 14 years later, post tenure and post promotion to Full Professor.

As I was teaching at the university level in those first years, I found there was nothing in the literature of educational leadership to connect me as a Black woman to who I was a leader and an educator. Thank God for the opportunity to meet, work with, and seek advice from two of the "firsts" in Educational Administration, Dr. Barbara Jackson at Fordham University and Dr. Flora Ida Ortiz at University of California-Riverside. All of the theories, concepts, examples, and stories were that of White males and occasionally White females. At UH, I had students from diverse populations and wanted them to be able to see themselves and their potential to be within the context of what I was teaching. I also wanted to tell the balanced story to those who were of the majority population, and I wanted to challenge their stereotypes and suppositions about the "other." The resistance to the "diverse" perspective and experience was so palpable in one course that I actually had two students (one White male and one Black female) almost come to blows when I used the "Who Should Be Hired?" decision-making exercise (Saldana, Norwood, & Alston, 2003) in an Introduction to School Administration course.

So, just as I had done with my dissertation on Black female superintendents, I began to search across the disciplines for supplemental teaching materials and information that would help to expand the field beyond the sea of Whiteness that was purported as the only truth. I was disappointed to find very little information, just as I had been with my dissertation. Thus, my frustration led to a *what if* moment. What if I wrote a book about Black women leaders that would not only add to the literature, but also speak to students, professors, and others on a personal level?

With that began the inquiry and the research for what would eventually become this book: *Herstories: Leading with the Lessons of the Lives of Black Women Activists*. The gestational process for this birth had periods of dormancy, but like the women who are presented in this text it needed time and its own refining period before it could be actualized.

I am a true believer in "things happen for a reason and when they're supposed to happen." So, it is no accident that this book is birthed at this point for this final iteration that has been produced. My time in academia has afforded me the opportunity to work with and mentor some of the best people and students that I could have ever asked for. I have co-presented and co-published with some outstanding students (i.e., those who could deal with the pressure of working with me and my expectations). One such student, Dr. Patrice McClellan, "my daughter," understood my drive to produce a work such as this. I met Patrice at Bowling Green State University in 2003. I remember her coming to my office to inquire about the Doctoral Program in Leadership Studies. I know that I can be intimidating (not on purpose) due to my expectations and my deep desire to provide high quality doctoral education. She weathered the storm through the application process, the coursework, and allowed me the opportunity to chair her dissertation. Her work on *Critical Servant Leadership* is a significant addition to the field of leadership and a unit of analysis for this text. Thus, I asked her to be the co-author. She will do great things in academia and I'm already proud of her.

This has been a spectacular journey and definitely worth the blood, sweat, and tears that have made this text what it is.

Judy A. Alston, Ph.D.
October 28, 2010

References

Saldana, D.C., Norwood, P.M., & Alston, J.A. (2003). Investigating teachers' unconscious person perceptions and stereotyping of culturally diverse individuals. *Educators for Urban Minorities*, 2, 57-73.

Acknowledgments

Gratitude is expressed to our respective institutions-Ashland University and Lourdes College-for allowing us time and space to complete this work; also special thank you's to Dr. Rochelle Brock (a fellow Penn Stater!) and Dr. Richard Johnson, III for their encouragement throughout this process.

Thanks to colleagues from across the country who have been sounding boards and supporters. Special thanks to our sisters in the *Scholarly Divas*: Dr. Lisa Bass, Dr. Karen Stansberry Beard, Dr. Cosette Grant, Dr. Sonya Douglass Horsford, Dr. April Peters, and Dr. Latish Reed.

Judy: Also special thanks to the Rev. Dr. Susan K. Smith and the supportive and encouraging family of Advent United Church of Christ, as well as to my wonderfully supportive sorors of the Columbus (OH) Alumnae Chapter of Delta Sigma Theta Sorority, Inc., as well as the continued love, friendship, support, and encouragement from my sorors who pledged the Epsilon Gamma chapter of Delta Sigma Theta Sorority, Inc. at The Pennsylvania State University, with whom I shared cherished times (and continued lifelong friendships) while I served as their advisor in the early '90s. Thanks and appreciation as well to my brothers and sister for life–Dr. Derrick Alridge (University of Georgia) from our undergraduate days at Winthrop College to teaching at Brookland-Cayce High School to doctoral student days at Penn State to now and still going strong; Dr. Larry Rowley (University of Michigan), and Dr. Catherine Lugg (Rutgers-The State University of New Jersey) for their love and support over the years and their respective historical scholarship that has majorly impacted the field.

CHAPTER ONE

Journey of Leadership

Leadership...is the indispensible social essence that gives common meaning to common purpose, that creates the incentive that makes other incentives effective, that infuses the subjective aspect of countless decisions with consistency in a changing environment, that inspires the personal conviction, that produces the vital cohesiveness without which cooperation is impossible. (Barnard, 1938, p. 283)

Leadership–The Context: In the Beginning

Leadership as a social phenomenon has been narrowly defined and researched from a White male hegemonic narrative (Allen, 1997; Nkomo, 1992; Parker, 2005; Parker & Olgivie, 1996). Consequently, traditional leadership theories as analyzed, taught, and researched are rarely generalizable to people of traditionally underrepresented groups, in particular Black women. We posit that Black women have what we call the "anomaly factor" in the minds of researchers, teachers, and aspirant leaders; which is the act of not linking the concept or ability of Black women to be pioneering leaders. For far too many, a Black woman leader is an oxymoronic concept. Historical accounts (hooks, 1984) of Black leadership dating back to slavery details the contributions of Black women in leadership roles inside and outside of the Black community. However, Black women are excluded from the studying and teaching of traditional leadership theories and concepts. In lieu of the exclusion of Black women from the leadership canonical discourse, we hypothesize that Black women's leadership in the United States has been a history of struggle for liberation, equality, and justice (Allen, 1997; Collins, 2000; Crawford, Rouse, & Woods, 1993; Lee, 2000; Robnett, 1996). Therefore, a goal of this text is to create inroads and extend the narrowly defined phenomenon of leadership to include and expand with the lens of Black women leadership.

In recent years there have been numerous studies and conceptual works on or about Black women's leadership experiences (Barnett, 1993; Blumberg, 1990; Brown, 1990; Clark, 1962; Collier-Thomas & Franklin, 2001; Collins, 1998, 2000; Crawford, et al., 1993; Davis, 1982; Grimes, 2005; hooks, 1981, 1984; Hull & Scott, 1982; Jean-Marie, Williams, & Sherman, 2009; Washington, 1992). A majority of such works have been biographical, descriptive, and more historical (Walters & Smith, 1999). This focused point of view, devoid of contextualization within traditional leadership theories, has led to more questions than answers regarding the type of leadership qualities and characteristics Black women possess. With much of the leadership and managerial literature developed by White men, and with many organizational theories based on observation of White male managers, it is not surprising that this focus on White male leaders' experiences promotes White male values as the behavioral managerial norm (Lamsa & Sintonen, 2001). However, there is a movement of scholarship that connects the biographical, descriptive, and historical experiences of Black women in the context of traditional leadership theories (Alston, 2000, 2005; Holvino, 2010; Parker, 2005; Parker & Olgivie, 1996). This book is a part of that movement. Although this movement is in an embryonic state (Walters & Smith, 1999), the work is promising.

Therefore, we situate our work on Black women in the context of critical servant leadership, transformational leadership, and social justice leadership. So given that we ask, what really is leadership and where do Black women fit–historically, theoretically, and in praxis?

Leadership Defined

Leadership is one of those words that elicits different reactions, perspectives, articulations, and definitions. There is no "one" way to definitively define a concept that is essential to us as human beings. Bennis (1959) stated:

> Always, it seems, the concept of leadership eludes us or turns up in
> another form to taunt us again with its slipperiness and complexity. So

we have invented an endless proliferation of terms to deal with it...and still the concept is not sufficiently defined. (p. 259)

Furthermore, Fleishman, Mumford, Zaccaro, Levin, Korotkin, and Hein (1991) noted that for over 60 years there have been as many as 65 different classification systems that have been developed to define the dimensions of leadership. Northouse (2007) made the point that while there are various ways to define leadership, there are four components that are identified as central to the concept:

- Leadership is a process;
- Leadership involves influence;
- Leadership occurs in a group context; and
- Leadership involves goal attainment. (p. 3)

Various definitions and thoughts of leadership include (but are not limited to) the following:

- "A leader is best when people barely know that he exists, not so good when people obey and acclaim him, worst when they despise him. 'Fail to honor people, they fail to honor you.' But of a good leader, who talks little, when his work is done, his aim fulfilled, they will all say, 'We did this ourselves.' " (Lao Tzu, *biographybase.com*)
- "A leader shapes and shares a vision which gives point to the work of others." (Handy, 1992)
- "A leader takes people where they want to go. A great leader takes people where they don't necessarily want to go, but ought to be." Rosalynn Carter, Former US First Lady, *buzzle.com*)
- "As we look ahead into the next century, leaders will be those who empower others." (Bill Gates, *ideachampions.com*)
- "Be willing to make decisions. That's the most important quality in a good leader." (General George S. Patton Jr., *leader-values.com*)
- "Leaders are individuals who establish direction for a working group of individuals who gain commitment from

these group members to this direction and who then motivate these members to achieve the direction's outcomes." (Conger, 1992, p. 18)

- "Leaders are those who consistently make effective contributions to social order, and who are expected and perceived to do so." (Hosking, 1988, p. 153)
- "Leadership (according to John Sculley) revolves around vision, ideas, direction, and has more to do with inspiring people as to direction and goals than with day-to-day implementation. A leader must be able to leverage more than his own capabilities. He must be capable of inspiring other people to do things without actually sitting on top of them with a checklist." (Bennis, 1989, p. 139)
- "Leadership and learning are indispensable to each other." (John F. Kennedy, *positivityblog.com*)
- Leadership is "a particular type of power relationship characterized by a group member's perception that another group member has the right to prescribe behavior patterns for the former regarding his activity as a group member." (Janda, 1960, p. 358)
- "Leadership is a combination of strategy and character. If you must be without one, be without the strategy." (Gen. H. Norman Schwarzkopf, *buzzle.com*)
- "Leadership is a development of a clear and complete system of expectations in order to identify, evoke and use the strengths of all resources in the organization the most important of which is people." (Batten, 1989 p. 35)
- "Leadership is a function of knowing yourself, having a vision that is well communicated, building trust among colleagues, and taking effective action to realize your own leadership potential." (Bennis, 1989)
- "Leadership is a process of giving purpose (meaningful direction) to collective effort, and causing willing effort to be expended to achieve purpose." (Jacobs & Jaques 1990, p.281)
- "Leadership is a process of influence between a leader and those who are followers." (Hollander, 1978, p.1)

- "Leadership is an attempt at influencing the activities of followers through the communication process and toward the attainment of some goal or goals." (Donelly, Ivancevich, & Gibson, 1985 p. 362.)
- "Leadership is an influence process that enable managers to get their people to do willingly what must be done, do well what ought to be done." (Cribbin, 1981)
- "Leadership is defined as the process of influencing the activities of an organized group toward goal achievement." (Rauch & Behling, 1984, p. 46)
- "Leadership is discovering the company's destiny and having the courage to follow it." (Joe Jaworski, as cited in Webber, 1996).
- "Leadership is influence–nothing more, nothing less." (Maxwell, 1998)
- "Leadership is interpersonal influence, exercised in a situation, and directed, through the communication process, toward the attainment of a specified goal or goals." (Tannenbaum, Weschler, & Massarik, 1961, p. 24)
- "Leadership is not a person or a position. It is a complex moral relationship between people, based on trust, obligation, commitment, emotion, and a shared vision of the good." (Ciulla, 1998)
- "Leadership is that process in which one person sets the purpose or direction for one or more other persons and gets them to move along together with him or her and with each other in that direction with competence and full commitment." (Jaques & Clement, 1994, p. 4)
- "Leadership is the accomplishment of a goal through the direction of human assistants. A leader is one who successfully marshals his human collaborators to achieve particular ends." (Prentice, 1961, p. 143)
- "Leadership is the art of influencing others to their maximum performance to accomplish any task, objective or project." (Cohen, 1990, p. 9)

- "Leadership is the art of mobilizing others to want to struggle for shared aspirations." (Kouzes & Posner, 1995, p. 30)
- "Leadership is the behavior of an individual when he is directing the activities of a group toward a shared goal." (Hemphill & Coons, 1957, p. 7)
- "Leadership is the capacity to translate vision into reality." (Bennis, 1989)
- "Leadership is the incremental influence that a person has beyond his or her formal authority." (Vecchio, 1988)
- "Leadership is the influential increment over and above mechanical compliance with the routine directives of the organization." (Katz & Kahn, 1978, p. 528)
- "Leadership is the initiation and maintenance of structure in expectation and interaction." (Stogdill, 1974, p. 411)
- "Leadership may be considered as the process (act) of influencing the activities of an organized group in its efforts toward goal setting and goal achievement." (Stogdill, 1950, p. 3)
- "Leadership requires using power to influence the thoughts and actions of other people." (Zalenik, 1992, p.126)
- "Management is efficiency in climbing the ladder of success; leadership determines whether the ladder is leaning against the right wall." (Covey, 2000)
- "People ask the difference between a leader and a boss...The leader works in the open, and the boss in covert. The leader leads, and the boss drives." (Theodore Roosevelt, *prabhal.com/leaders*)
- "The final test of a leader is that he leaves behind in others the conviction and will to carry on." (Walter Lippman, *buzzle.com*)
- "The first responsibility of a leader is to define reality. The last is to say thank you. In between the two, the leader must become a servant and a debtor. That sums up the progress of an artful leader." (Max DePree, *leadervalues.com*)

- "The function of leadership is to produce more leaders, not more followers." (Ralph Nader, *thinkexist.com*)
- "The growth and development of people is the highest calling of leadership." (H S. Firestone, *leadervalues.com*)
- "The job of the leader is to speak to the possibility." (Zander, 2001)
- "The key to successful leadership today is influence, not authority." (K. Blanchard, *inspirationalquotes4u.com*)
- "The only definition of a leader is someone who has followers." (Drucker, 2003)
- "You manage things, you lead people." (Admiral Grace Murray Hooper, U. S. Naval officer, *ianscotland.com*)
- "A leader is the person in a group who directs and coordinates task-oriented group activities." (Fiedler, 1967)
- "Leaders are those who consistently make effective contributions to social order and who are expected and perceived to do so." (Hosking, 1988)
- "Leadership is a social process in which one individual influences the behavior of others without the use of threat or violence." (Buchanan & Huczynski, 1997, p. 606)
- "Leadership is about articulating visions, embodying values, and creating the environment within which things can be accomplished." (Richards & Engel, 1986, p. 206)
- "Leadership is the ability to step outside the culture to start evolutionary change processes that are more adaptive." (Schein, 1992, p. 2)
- "Leadership is the creation of a vision about a desired future state which seeks to enmesh all members of an organization in its net." (Bryman, 1986, p. 6)
- "Leadership is the lifting of a man's vision to higher sights, the raising of a man's performance to a higher standard, the building of a man's personality beyond its normal limitations." (Drucker, 2003)
- "Leadership is the process of influencing the activities of an individual or a group in efforts toward goal achievement in a given situation." (Hersey & Blanchard, 1988, p. 86)

- "Leadership is the process of making sense of what people are doing together so that people will understand and be committed." (Drath & Palus, 1994, p. 4)
- "...the art of getting someone else to do something you want done because he wants to do it." (Dwight D Eisenhower, *positivityblog.com*)
- "One of the hardest tasks of leadership is understanding that you are not what you are, but what you're perceived to be by others." (Edward L. Flom, CEO of the Florida Steel Corporation, *decision-making-solutions.com*)
- "Leadership is all hype. We've had three great leaders in this century - Hitler, Stalin and Mao." (Drucker, 2003)
- "Leadership is an intangible quality with no clear definition. That's probably a good thing, because if the people who were being led knew the definition, they would hunt down their leaders and kill them." (Adams, 1996)
- "Leadership: The capacity and will to rally people to a common purpose together with the character that inspires confidence and trust." (Field Marshal Montgomery, *thepracticeofleadership.net*)
- "A Leader: A person responsible for achieving objectives through others by creating the conditions in which they may be successful and for building and maintaining the team that he or she is a member of." (Jeremy Tozer, *strategicleadership.com.au*)
- "Leadership should be born out of the understanding of the needs of those who would be affected by it." (Marian Anderson, *leadership501.com*)
- "Leadership is an influence relationship among leaders and followers who intend real changes that reflect their mutual purposes." (Rost, 1993, p. 102)

Leadership can also be defined as the process of influencing one or more people in a positive way so that the tasks determined by the goals and objectives of an organization are accomplished. The leadership role can either be assigned or assumed. It has a complex blend of behaviors, attitudes, and values; leadership can occur in a small organization where everyone is known or in a complex bureaucracy where few people even in a department know each other (Hart, 1980). Most often, researchers have defined leadership according to their own individual perspectives and aspects of this phenomenon that have been of most interest to them. Leadership has also been defined in terms of individual behavior, influence over other people, interaction patterns, role relationships, occupation of an administrative position, and perception of others regarding legitimacy of influence (Yukl, 2009). Other researchers have defined leadership as a characteristic or distinguishing feature, quality, or attribute possessed by people that enables them to effectively accomplish goals (Cook, 1930; Tead; 1930).

Leadership is a concept central to theories of how organizations such as educational bureaucracies work (Blackmore, 1989). In recent years, leadership has been viewed more of as a process and has included the concepts of creating action, promoting empowerment and growth, or involving the interaction between leaders and followers. Another aspect of leadership as a process is the interaction between leaders and followers. More recently, the newer definitions of leadership demand rethinking the traditional images and the traditional relationships associated with leaders and followers (Green, 1997).

According to Davis (2003), the term leadership implies movement, taking the organization or some part of it in a new direction, solving problems, being creative, initiating new programs, building organizational structures, and improving quality (p. 4). The research of Bass and Stogdill (1990) reported on more than 3,000 empirical investigations of leadership, which provided varied conceptions of what leadership means. Given the many perspectives on leadership, Birnbaum (1992) noted, "Any comprehensive consideration of academic leadership must be able to accommodate both the strong leader and the weak leader views, because evidence suggests that while both may be incomplete, both are in some measure correct" (p. 8).

From another vantage point, Owens (1995) noted that leadership is group function and that leaders purposely seek to influence the behavior of others. A newer view of leadership looks at the concept as a process in which leaders are not seen as individuals in charge of followers, but as members who make meaning in a community of practice (Drath & Palus, 1994; Horner, 1997). Leadership is taking risks, making mistakes, and learning from these mistakes. It provides the solid foundation on which the organization can thrive. When leadership is right, people are inspired to do their best.

Various qualifications, attributes, characteristics, and skills have been studied and described by researchers on what makes an effective or successful leader (Alston, 1999; Alston & Jones, 2002; Chapman, 1993; Sergiovanni, 1996; Zhang, 1994). Rost (1991) noted that traditional leadership scholars and the theories they developed were concerned with the peripheries of leadership, such as traits, personality characteristics, and whether leaders are born or made. Furthermore, scholars are interested in the components of leadership and what leaders need to know to be influential in an organization. Less research has been "aimed at understanding the essential nature of what leadership is, and the processes whereby leaders and followers relate to one another to achieve a purpose" (p. 4).

In this 21st century, what should leadership mean? What should it look like? Parker (2005) presented a (re)interpretation of leadership for this time, combining the leadership as a process of social construction and a focus on social change via dialogic interaction:

> Leadership is an influence relationship among leaders and followers who intend real changes that reflect their mutual purposes (Rost, 1991); and these mutual purposes are negotiated through a process whereby one or more individuals (leaders and followers) succeeds in attempting to frame and define the reality of others. (Smircich & Morgan, 1982, p. 26)

Given this, it is important and needed to study, examine, and unpack this social construction of the concept of leadership in this 21st century, particularly within the changing meanings of race and gender.

Seminal Studies of Leadership

From a historical context, there are the seminal studies of leadership that undergird the discipline of leadership in general. Between the 1930s and the 1950s well-known and oft-cited behavior studies were conducted at the University of Iowa, The Ohio State University, and the University of Michigan.

The Iowa Studies (Lewin, Lippitt, & White, 1939) conducted group studies using three styles of leadership identified as autocratic, laissez-faire, and democratic. The autocratic leader holds decision-making responsibilities, is very direct, and power resides with this individual. The laissez-faire leader is one who concedes decision-making power to others; this person chooses a hands-off approach. The democratic leader allows for a space of shared decision-making. Lewin, Lippitt, and White found this third type to be the most effective. In recent years, the democratic style has been included in the work of Goleman, Boyatzis, and McKee (2002) as one of their six emotional leadership styles: visionary, coaching, affiliative, democratic, pacesetting, and commanding. Here Goleman and colleagues view leadership as primal as it is at its core rooted in emotions. Thus, the fundamental job of a leader is to prime good feelings in those they lead. Leaders who excel in this create what they call *resonance*—a reservoir of positivity that unleashes the best in people

Beginning in the 1950s, at The Ohio State University a series of studies (Stogdill & Coons, 1957; Stodgill, 1974, 1981; Fleishman, 1953; Hemphill & Coons, 1950) on leadership were conducted. Using the Leaders Behavior Description Questionnaire (LBDQ) and the Supervisor Behavior Description Questionnaire (SBDQ), they found that there were two important characteristics for leadership: consideration and initiating structure. Consideration is the degree to which a leader acts in a friendly and supportive manner towards subordinates. Initiating Structure is the degree to which a leader defines and structures her or his role as well as the roles of the subordinates toward achieving the goals of the organization.

Also during the 1950s, under the direction of Rensis Likert (1958), researchers at the University of Michigan were conducting leadership research. The focus of the Michigan studies was to determine the principles and methods of leadership that led to productivity and job satisfaction. The studies resulted in two general leadership behaviors or orientations: an employee orientation and a production orientation. Leaders with an employee orientation showed genuine concern for interpersonal relations. Those with a production orientation focused on the task or technical aspects of the job. The Michigan Studies concluded that an employee orientation and general instead of close supervision yielded better results. Likert (1961, 1979) later developed four "systems" of management based on these studies. The four systems are labeled 1) Exploitive Authoritative (compared to McGregor's Theory X type of leadership); 2) Benevolent Authoritative (carrot stick method); 3) Consultative; and 4) Participative. He advocated for System 4 (the participative-group system, which was the most participatory set of leader behaviors) as resulting in the most positive outcomes.

Robert Blake and Jane Mouton (1964) developed the Managerial Grid, which utilized the *concern for people* versus *concern for production* dichotomy proposed by both the Ohio State and the University of Michigan studies. This model originally identified five different leadership styles based on the *concern for people* and the *concern for production*; these two dimensions served as axes of leadership orientation. The five styles were: Authoritarian Leader (high task, low relationship), Team Leader (high task, high relationship), Country Club Leader (low task, high relationship), Impoverished Leader (low task, low relationship and Middle of the Road Management (maintains status quo). In later years Robert Blake and Ann Adams McCanse (1991) updated the grid and the new grid identified seven new styles, which they found to be the most important differences among leaders:

- Control and Dominate (Dictatorial)
- Yield and Support (Accommodating)
- Balance and Compromise (Status Quo)
- Evade and Elude (Indifferent)
- Prescribe and Guide (Paternalistic)
- Exploit and Manipulate (Opportunistic)
- Contribute and Commit (Sound)

Interestingly, Blake completed this major research with two women as his co-researchers though gender is not a consideration in the research itself.

While leadership in the organization (Peterson, 1997), team leadership (Bensimon & Neumann, 1993), servant leadership (Greenleaf, 1977; Spears & Lawrence, 2003), transformative leadership (Burns, 1978), inclusive leadership (Helgesen, 1995), and the role of followership (Kelley, 1998) have replaced the traditional discussions of the great man leader, the great man leadership theory is still held in high regard. The "great man" leadership theory purported that leaders were men born with particular traits. This concept of leadership often elicits images of powerful, charismatic persons who are most often White and male. Weber (1947) defined charisma as a certain quality of an individual personality, by virtue of which s/he is set apart from ordinary people and treated as endowed with supernatural, superhuman, or at least specifically exceptional powers or qualities. These are such as are not accessible to the ordinary person, but are regarded as of divine origin or as exemplary, and on the basis of them the individual concerned is treated as a leader. It is the type of leadership that is generated by great moments of social instability and unrest, wherein the charismatic leader challenges the status quo by evoking the deepest emotions and energies of his audience (Marable, 1998). The names are familiar: Abraham Lincoln, John F. Kennedy, Bill Gates, William Jefferson Clinton, Adolf Hitler, Winston Churchill, Julius Caesar, Benjamin Franklin, Thomas Alva Edison, Alexander Graham Bell, Henry Ford, Orville and Wilbur Wright, Franklin Delano Roosevelt, Steve Jobs, Vince Lombardi, and Douglas MacArthur. Other male leaders who were men of color include Mohandas Karamchand Gandhi, Rev. Dr. Martin Luther King, Jr., Nelson Mandela, Malcolm X (born Malcolm Little and later known and died as El-Hajj Malik El-Shabazz), and Steve Biko. This trait theory view is that leaders possess certain traits that are natural and make them prone to success. Thomas Carlyle (1869) in his book *Heroes and Hero Worship* researched the traits and leadership of such men as Jesus Christ, Muhammad, Shakespeare, Martin Luther, Napoleon Bonaparte. While research (Stogdill, 1948) and time have challenged that this trait theory approach is universal and preeminent, it is still a very well known view of leadership.

Another category of leadership theory houses the contingency or situational theories of leadership, which propose that the organizational or work group context affects the extent to which given leader traits and behaviors will be effective. Contingency theory, based on adaptations of the organization and the environment, is the notion that effective leadership is contingent on a compatible relationship between the leader's style/qualities and the context in which the person is leading. In other words, as noted by Northouse (2007), "effective leadership is contingent on matching a leader's style to the right setting (situation)" (p. 113). Contingency theory helps to place leadership in a social context. Four of the more well-known contingency theories are Fiedler's contingency theory, path-goal theory, the Vroom, Yetton and Yago decision-making model of leadership, and the situational leadership theory.

Fiedler's (1964, 1967) work is the foundation upon which contingency theory is built. He proposed a contingency model to predict leadership effectiveness by using the Least Preferred Coworker (LPC) Scale. The LPC is an instrument for measuring an individual's leadership orientation. The scale asks a leader to think of all the people with whom they have ever worked and then describe the person with whom they have worked least well, The leader was asked to grade their least favorite worker on a series of bipolar adjectives (pleasant versus unpleasant, friendly versus unfriendly, gloomy versus cheerful, etc.), with the scales designed so that the most lenient leader would receive the highest LPC score. A high LPC score suggests that the leader has a human relations orientation, while a low LPC score indicates a task orientation. Fiedler (1974) identified three contingencies that are prevalent in every leadership situation:

1. The relationship between the leader and group members, which can be of a good or poor quality. The leader who is respected by the group enjoys considerable power and has little need of official rank or sanctions to get things done.

2. The tasks structure, which can be either structured or unstructured. Unstructured tasks make it more difficult for the leader to exercise influence since neither the leader nor the followers can be dogmatic about what should be done.
3. Position power of the leader, which can be high or low. There is power invested in the leader's position distinct from any personal power achieved through skillful handling of group relationship. (as cited in Norton, 2005, p. 34)

The second well-known contingency theory is "Path-Goal Theory." House's path-goal conceptualization of leadership used Vroom's (1964) expectancy theory of motivation to identify the effects of leader behavior on subordinate outcome variables. Defined by House (1971) and House and Mitchell (1974), the theory states that a leader's behavior is contingent on the satisfaction, motivation, and performance of his subordinates. House and Mitchell (as cited on changingminds.org) describe four styles of leadership:

- Supportive Leadership: Considering the needs of the follower, showing concern for their welfare and creating a friendly working environment. This includes increasing the follower's self-esteem and making the job more interesting. This approach is best when the work is stressful, boring or hazardous.
- Directive Leadership: Telling followers what needs to be done and giving appropriate guidance along the way. This includes giving them schedules of specific work to be done at specific times. Rewards may also be increased as needed and role ambiguity decreased (by telling them what they should be doing). This may be used when the task is unstructured and complex and the follower is inexperienced. This increases the follower's sense of security and control and hence is appropriate to the situation.
- Participative Leadership: Consulting with followers and taking their ideas into account when making decisions and taking particular actions. This approach is best when the

followers are expert and their advice is both needed and they expect to be able to give it.

- Achievement-oriented Leadership: Setting challenges and goals, both in their work and in self-improvement. High standards are demonstrated and expected. The leader shows faith in the capabilities of the follower to succeed. This approach is best when the task is complex.

House (1996) later reformulated the theory to include eight classes of leader behavior, with the theory's essence being that "leaders, to be effective, engage in behaviors that complement subordinates' environments and abilities in a manner that compensates for deficiencies and is instrumental to subordinate satisfaction and individual and work unit performance" (p. 323).

Another contingency theory by Vroom and Yetton (1973) described what leaders should do in certain situations concerning the level of decision-making involvement of followers. A decision tree that inquired about the need for participation was utilized in the process, and a conclusion could then be drawn about the level of followers' involvement in order for the leader to be most effective. This model, known as the normative decision model, placed the leader into one of five levels of participation: autocratic, in which the leader solved the problem or made the decision without followers' involvement; informed-autocratic, defined as solving the problem after obtaining relative information from followers; individual-consultative, in which the leader shared the problem and sought input from individuals, then made a decision which may or may not have reflected the influence of subordinates; group-consultative, in which a group was formed, the problem was shared with the group, the group's ideas were sought, and the leader made the final decision; and group-agreement, in which followers understood the problem and worked with the leader to reach consensus on a solution.

Additionally, it is important to note that within the *traditional* leadership discussions and theories, women have not been highlighted. One notable exception of gender-biased theory is the Hersey and Blanchard (1977) Situational Leadership model where gender is a consideration. Originally called the "life cycle theory of leadership," this theoretical model posits that the developmental levels of a leader's subordinates play the greatest role in determining which leadership styles are most appropriate (leader behaviors). According to this conceptualization, leader behaviors fall along two continua, (1) directive behavior, and (2) supportive behavior. These two continua involve the following styles:

- Delegating Style—allowing the group to take responsibility for task decisions; this is a low-task, low-relationship style.
- Participating Style—emphasizing shared ideas and participative decisions on task directions; this is a low-task, high-relationship style.
- Selling Style—explaining task directions in a supportive and persuasive way; this is a high-task, high-relationship style.
- Telling Style—giving specific task directions and closely supervising work; this is a high-task, low-relationship style.

Hersey and Blanchard believed that leaders should be flexible and adjust their styles as followers and situations change over time.

Gender, Race, and Leadership

It had not been until the late 20th century that literature on leadership made gender an observable factor. There have been some studies that suggested that there are differences between male and female leaders, while others suggested that there are no significant differences (Adkinson, 1981; Frasher & Frasher, 1979; Shakeshaft, 1989). Research on gender and leadership has found some interesting results. For example, in 1978, Hollander and Yoder concluded that there were general areas where men and women differ in leadership: 1) men focus more on achieving success in tasks while women seek interpersonal success; 2) men focus on displaying recognizable leader behavior while women focus on creating a positive group effort. They concluded that differences were related to role expectations, style, and situational characteristics.

In the 1970s researchers started to investigate the role of gender difference in leadership. Yet and still, most of the characteristics that are associated with leadership are those with masculine connotations. These masculine connotations and identities are therefore seen to characterize leadership and management dynamics. Martin's (1996) research, for example, illustrates this by highlighting that formal and informal decision-making processes are traditionally dominated by men and therefore reproduce qualities associated with masculinity. Wacjman (1998) also noted that dominant masculinities are manifested in managerial competencies that favor what she calls action-man-type qualities. In other words, male leaders are stereotypically seen as confident, rational, and strong. Female leaders are stereotypically seen as passive, nurturing, and relationship-oriented (Helgeson, 1990). One size does not fit all. It is in the period of the 1980s where women began to challenge the idea that terms "masculine" and "leadership" were synonymous. Gilligan (1980) made it clear that men's experiences cannot be generalized to women and Belenky et al. (1986), Bensimon (1989), and others have written of the connected mode of leadership for women, which includes the interdependence of love and care.

Helgesen's (1990) *The Feminine Advantage* described the "feminine principles of management" which are characterized as principles of caring, making intuitive decisions, and viewing leadership from a nonhierarchical perspective. The central thesis for Helgesen was that women have skill in building relationships and that is better for business than the traditional hierarchical model wherein power is given to a small few. Some literature on women's leadership suggests more sharing of power and a participatory orientation to leading (Chliwniak, 1997; Townsend & Twombly, 1998). Stereotypically, the feminine style of leadership (consideration or people-oriented) is characterized by nurturing of interpersonal relationships. In a stereotypical masculine leadership style (initiating structure or task-oriented), task performance and achievement of organizational goals is emphasized. These styles relate to gender because of the stereotypes people have of men as instrumental, competent, rational and assertive (masculinity) and of women as sensitive, warm, tactful and expressive (femininity) (e.g. Broverman, Vogel,

Broverman, Clarkson, & Rosenkrantz, 1972; Deaux & Lewis, 1984). Thus, the more instrumental, task-oriented, autocratic styles are therefore often referred to as masculine leadership styles and the interpersonal-oriented, charismatic, and democratic styles as feminine leadership styles (Klenke, 1996). Yet, these female-oriented leadership characteristics have been hailed, though without fanfare, as successful by various researchers and popular authors (Peters & Waterman, 1984; Senge, 1990, 1994; Collins, 2001).

The absence and silence of women in leadership is perpetuated by the contention that women are trying to be leaders inside hierarchical organizations that promote gender stratification by roles and maintain values and beliefs based on men's experience. In other words, they are determined to lead in a space that was not designed for them to lead or be successful. Unfortunately this stratification and the gender stereotypes leave women with a double standard and in a double bind (Kellerman & Rhode, 2007). This incongruence creates social tension for women in leadership (Hart, 1995). It is here that women find themselves "wedged into stereotypes, often acting against female values, trying to fit the male definition of leadership" (Wilson, 2004, p. 3). Given this, the concept of "post-heroic leadership" has found its way into the discussion of women and leadership. Coined by Huey (1994), this implicit philosophy assumes that leadership rests in individuals who must be capable of inspiring and influencing others to solve problems and achieve goals. This type of leadership is based on bottom-up transformation fueled by shared power and community building. However, this so-called "heroic" view of leadership is often based on a deficiency view of people, as Peter Senge (1990) noted,

> Especially in the West, leaders are heroes-great men (and occasionally women) who rise to the fore' in times of crises... At its heart, the traditional view of leadership is based on assumptions of people's powerlessness, their lack of personal vision and inability to master the forces of change, deficits which can be remedied only by a few great leaders. (p. 340)

Fletcher (2004) noted that it involves three ideals: Leadership as practice: shared and distributed; leadership as social process: interactions; and leadership as learning: outcomes. All of these are most often associated with the "female leadership" style or women's ways of leading (Gilligan, 1982). As Parker (2005) furthered,

> The central argument, however, is that the feminine style, grounded in female values such as relationship-building, interdependence, and being other-focused, is better suited than the male hierarchical approach to leading contemporary complex organizing contexts, but it is stifled by current, male-dominated structuring that values hierarchy, independence, and self-efficacy processes. (pp. 9-10)

While much of the literature on leadership ignores women, either by making the assumption that leaders are male or by assuming a "gender-free" position, it also ignores the issue of race, specifically Black women. Though studies of women leaders have increased in number, specific studies of women in leadership and scholarly inquiries related to Black women remain rare (Alston, 2003, 2005). Black women are poorly represented in leadership positions (Alston, 2000; Jean-Marie, et al., 2009) and in the knowledge base itself; they are vastly underrepresented in the actual content of leadership courses and texts. Banks (2001) suggested that one dimension of an inclusive curriculum in content integration–the use of examples and content from a variety of cultures and groups to illustrate key concepts, principles, generalizations, and theories in their subject and/or discipline. There is a problematic approach in studies of leadership which omit the perspectives of "raced people"–individuals who "have faced discrimination because of race and/or class, and have been oppressed psychologically, physically, educationally, or economically" (Tate, 1997). Without such culturally inclusive perspectives, the field of leadership will not benefit from the unique experiences of raced people. In addition, without such perspectives current theories of leadership remain narrow in scope, lacking a more inclusive frame noting the particular shortcomings as they apply to raced people (as cited in Gooden, 2002, p. 135).

The reality is that there has been race-neutral theorizing (Parker, 2005) in the study of leadership. White male privilege has been the standard to define, research, and report about leadership. African American women do not fit neatly in these various models of leadership as presented. Understanding the intersections of work and family in Black women's lives is key to clarifying the overarching economy of domination and leadership (Collins, 2008). Black women have been addressing the concerns of White male domination and hegemony from the very beginning. Sojourner Truth's question "Ain't I a Woman?" still rings true, as bell hooks (1999) notes, "we can and do speak for ourselves. And our struggle is to be heard" (p. 43).

Black Women and the Path to Leadership: A Historical Perspective

> The male-dominated gender politics of uplift posed difficulties for Black women as race leaders...Black women are thus placed in the subordinate position of sacrificing gender consciousness and their reproductive self-determination in the name of race unity. In other ways, this male orientation affected how Black oppression was theorized, emphasizing the victimization of Black men through lynching or economic exclusion and silencing the particular victimization of Black women. (Gaines, 1993, p. 13)

While we have come a long way and some things have indeed changed, yet, many believe that Black women and leadership are oxymoronic terms; they are not. African American women's organizational leadership dates back to the time of slavery and forward into the civil rights movement (Payne, 1995). More pointedly, Parker (2005) argued "in the era of slavery that the seeds were planted for the emergence of African American women's tradition of leadership" (p. 33). Today's Black female leaders stand on the shoulders of the many unnamed women who paved the path with their lives. The 21st century Black woman leader continues to espouse and embody the essence of her Black foremother leaders in that she continues to: 1) be self-defined, 2) be self-determined, 3) develop and use her voice, 4) connect to and build community, and 5) seek spirituality and regeneration (Parker, 2005).

Most often when reading about Black women in positions of leadership one will find that these women were often leaders in the context of education and grassroots organizing. Throughout history it has been evident that the Black female has pioneered new frontiers in education as leaders as well as participants (Rusher, 1996). For example, a specific view of Black woman classroom leaders finds that prior to the 1954 *Brown* decision, approximately 82,000 Black teachers taught two million Black children who attended mostly segregated schools (Hudson & Holmes, 1994; Toppo, 2004). In segregated Black schools of the south before the decision, Henig, Hula, Orr, and Pedescleaux (1999) noted that Black teachers and principals were important role models and respected leaders in their communities. Tillman (2004) furthered that teaching was a noteworthy and important profession in the Black community and served as a primary leadership particularly for Black women (Ethridge, 1979; Foster, 1997; Yeakey, Johnston, & Adkison, 1986). Unfortunately Black women did not have real status in the teaching profession until the late 19th century (Shakeshaft, 1989). Women such as Fannie Jackson Coppin, Lucy Laney, Charlotte Hawkins Brown, and Fannie Barrier Williams began their careers as southern elementary teachers.

Many of these Black teachers and administrators were Jeanes supervisors. For over 60 years these master teachers traveled throughout the south to provide education and other related services to poor Black children. Eighty percent of these supervisors were Black women (Guthrie-Jordan, 1990), and thus the precursor to the modern-day Black female superintendent. These women were chosen because they were "self-effacing, stimulating others to put forth their best effort rather than making... [themselves] too active or too prominent" (Brawley, 1971, p. 62); they were perceived to be less threatening. Female Jeanes supervisors did face similar problems that working women have always faced and that African-American often face in their relationship with White men—those being issues of power, gender, and race (Botsch, 1996; Smith, 1997). This fact is also supported by the work of Doughty (1980), Ortiz (1982), and Korah (1990) who all conclude that minority women, in fact, do confront the barriers of race and gender as they endeavor to achieve positions of leadership.

The leadership strategies and tactics used in the Black Women's Club Movement became the foundation for the leadership practices of the Black women leaders in civil rights movement of the 1960s. Many Black women held positions of leadership, most often out of the limelight. They were the invisible leaders and backbone of the movements (Apatheker, 1982; Hine & Thompson, 1998; Payne, 1995). In *How Long? How Long? African American Women in the Struggle for Civil Rights*, Belinda Robnett (1997) provided a sociological analysis of Black women's leadership in various civil rights campaigns. She argued that Black women in leadership positions were often serving as the bridge (her "woman bridge leader" concept) between local civil rights struggles and national protest organizations. Thus, they operated on local levels, established the links and connections with grassroots organizations, which in turn provided mass support for the civil rights goals and objectives (Collier-Thomas & Franklin, 2001).

When the roll is called up yonder, the names for many still here will be familiar but more often unfamiliar, yet they all *led* and laid the foundation for Black women leader herstories. They are (but are not limited to):

- Amy Jacques Garvey–a leading Pan-Africanist and Black Nationalist worked with her husband Marcus Garvey to advance the cause of Black liberation; journalist, feminist and race activist.
- Anna Easter Brown–Alpha Kappa Alpha Sorority, Inc. founder; educator, writer.
- Anna Julia Cooper–teacher, principal, scholar; fourth African American woman to receive a Ph.D. in the United States.
- Beulah Burke–Alpha Kappa Alpha Sorority, Inc. founder; dedicated Home Economics teacher; civic activist.
- Lillie Burke–Alpha Kappa Alpha Sorority, Inc. founder; educator in English in academic programs in public high schools in Pennsylvania, and especially Washington, DC, where she spent most of her career; head of the academic department at Downing Institute in Pennsylvania; taught at the State Normal School at Fayetteville (NC).
- Bernice Johnson Reagon–activist, singer, scholar, composer; founder of *Sweet Honey in the Rock*.

- Bertha Pitts Campbell–Delta Sigma Theta Sorority, Inc. founder, participated in the 1913 Women's Suffrage March; Seattle civil rights worker; was a founder of the Christian Friends for Racial Equality.
- Betty Shabazz–educator, nurse, civil rights activist; associate professor of health sciences with a concentration in nursing at New York's Medgar Evers College; Director of Institutional Advancement and Public Affairs at Medgar Evers College.
- Bridget "Biddy" Mason–ex-slave; nurse/midwife; a successful entrepreneur, philanthropist; one of first Black women to own land in Los Angeles.
- Charity Adams Early–first Black woman to be commissioned as an officer in the Women's Army Corps (WAC); retired after the war as the highest ranking Black officer in the service.
- Charlene Alexander Mitchell–international socialist, feminist, labor and civil rights activist; stood as a third-party candidate in the 1968 United States presidential election.
- Connie Matthews–activist, Black Panther Party International coordinator.
- Dorothy I. Height–educator, activist; president of the National Council of Negro Women for 40 years; 10th National President of Delta Sigma Theta Sorority, Inc.
- Edith Motte Young–Delta Sigma Theta Sorority, Inc. founder, participated in the 1913 Women's Suffrage March; 1st Recording Secretary for the sorority; accomplished pianist.
- Edna Brown Coleman–Delta Sigma Theta Sorority, Inc. founder, participated in the 1913 Women's Suffrage March; president and valedictorian of the 1913 graduating class at Howard University.
- Eliza Pearl Shippen–Delta Sigma Theta Sorority, Inc. founder, participated in the 1913 Women's Suffrage March; received her M.A. from the Teachers College of Columbia University and Ph.D. from the University of Pennsylvania.

- Ethel Carr Watson–Delta Sigma Theta Sorority, Inc. founder, participated in the 1913 Women's Suffrage March; NY; teacher; dramatic performer.
- Ethel Cuff Black–Delta Sigma Theta Sorority, Inc. founder, participated in the 1913 Women's Suffrage March; first Black teacher in Richmond County, NY; community affairs activist.
- Ethel Hedgeman Lyle – Alpha Kappa Alpha Sorority, Inc. founder; educator; was the first African-American female college graduate to teach in a normal school in Oklahoma and the first to earn a Teacher's Life Certificate from the Oklahoma State Department of Education.
- Florence Letcher Toms–Delta Sigma Theta Sorority, Inc. founder, participated in the 1913 Women's Suffrage March; lifelong educator, assistant principal.
- Fredrica Chase Dodd–Delta Sigma Theta Sorority, Inc. founder, participated in the 1913 Women's Suffrage March; educator, social worker, activist; one of New York's first Black social workers.
- Gloria Richardson–the leader of the Cambridge Movement, a civil rights struggle in Cambridge, Maryland in the 1960s. The Movement made significant strides against institutionalized racial discrimination in Cambridge by bringing attention to social injustices such as inadequate wages, poor housing, and poor health care.
- H. Louise Mouzon–graduate of Avery Normal Institute in Charleston, SC; one of the first Black public school teachers in Charleston; 37 years teaching at Burke High School.
- Ida B. Wells Barnett–anti-lynching crusader, suffragist, women's rights advocate, journalist, and speaker.
- Jessie McGuire Dent–Delta Sigma Theta Sorority, Inc. founder, participated in the 1913 Women's Suffrage March; educator, activists; successfully sued for equal pay for Black teachers in Galveston, TX.
- Jimmie Bugg Middleton–Delta Sigma Theta Sorority, Inc. founder, participated in the 1913 Women's Suffrage March;

teacher, librarian, Dean of Girls; president and national treasurer of National Association of College Women.

- Joan Little–the first woman in United States' history to be acquitted using the defense that she used deadly force to resist sexual assault; authored a poem entitled "I Am Somebody."
- Joanna Mary Berry Shields–Alpha Kappa Alpha Sorority, Inc. founder; educator; civic leader.
- June Johnson–was just 15 years old and an original member of the Student Nonviolent Coordinating Committee when she was arrested in Winona, Mississippi on June 11, 1963, on her way back from a voter registration training course with a handful of other activists and was beaten and jailed in Mississippi in one of the most savage incidents in the Civil Rights Movement.
- Karen Galloway Bethea-Shields–the first African-American woman ever to graduate from Duke Law School. The day she passed the bar exam, she was named Jerry Paul's co-counsel in his defense of Joan Little, who was acquitted of all charges.
- Kathleen Cleaver–Law professor; Black Panther activist.
- Lavinia Norman–Alpha Kappa Alpha Sorority, Inc. founder; 40-year educator.
- Lucy Diggs Slowe–Alpha Kappa Alpha Sorority, Inc. founder; appointed the first Dean of Women at Howard University. She continued as a college administrator at Howard for 15 years; in 1917, the first African-American woman to win a major sports title (tennis).
- Madree Penn White–Delta Sigma Theta Sorority, Inc. founder, participated in the 1913 Women's Suffrage March; first female editor of the *Howard University Journal*; journalist; formed the Triangle Press Company, publishing and printing firm in St. Louis.
- Mamie Reddy Rose – Delta Sigma Theta Sorority, Inc. founder, participated in the 1913 Women's Suffrage March.
- Margaret Flagg-Holmes – Alpha Kappa Alpha Sorority, Inc. founder; earned a master's in Philosophy at Columbia

University; devoted her energies to teaching academic, or college preparatory curriculum at the high school level for more than thirty years, mostly in Chicago, Illinois. She was voted "Best Latin Teacher" in Chicago; led the history department at Du Sable High School for several years.

- Marguerite Young Alexander–Delta Sigma Theta Sorority, Inc. founder, participated in the 1913 Women's Suffrage March; French and Spanish correspondence secretary for a Chicago firm.
- Marie Woolfolk Taylor–Alpha Kappa Alpha Sorority, Inc. founder; social worker and probation officer and chaired numerous civic groups.
- Marjorie Hill–Alpha Kappa Alpha Sorority, Inc. founder; educator.
- Mary Ellen Pleasants–called "the Mother of Civil Rights in California"; former bonded servant.
- Myra Davis Hemmings–Delta Sigma Theta Sorority, Inc. founder, participated in the 1913 Women's Suffrage March; 1st president of Delta Sigma Theta Sorority, Inc. (and Alpha Kappa Alpha before the split); teacher, orator, writer.
- Naomi Sewell Richardson – Delta Sigma Theta Sorority, Inc. founder, participated in the 1913 Women's Suffrage March; first Black graduate of Washingtonville High School (NY); educator; community activist.
- Olive C. Jones–Delta Sigma Theta Sorority, Inc. founder, participated in the 1913 Women's Suffrage March; music teacher.
- Osceola Macarthy Adams–Delta Sigma Theta Sorority, Inc. founder, participated in the 1913 Women's Suffrage March; educator, actress, director; Director of the Harlem School for the Arts.
- Pat Parker–lesbian, feminist, poet, activist; founded the Black Women's Revolutionary Council; contributed to the formation of the Women's Press Collective, as well as being involved in wide-ranging activism in gay and lesbian organizing.

- Pauline Oberdorfer Minor–Delta Sigma Theta Sorority, Inc. founder, participated in the 1913 Women's Suffrage March; educator; 1914 valedictorian at Howard University; mezzo-soprano soloist; hymn writer; taught at Avery Normal Institute in Charleston, SC.
- Ruby Doris Smith Robinson–served SNCC as an activist in the field and as an administrator in the Atlanta central office. She eventually succeeded James Forman as SNCC's executive secretary and was the only woman ever to serve in this capacity.
- Ruth Ellis – was the oldest known open lesbian, and an LGBT rights activist; died at age 101; first American woman to own a printing business in Detroit.
- Rutha Mae Harris – activist; original Freedom Singer; member of Sweet Honey in the Rock.
- Sarah "Sadie" Green Oglesby–graduate of Avery Normal Institute in Charleston, SC; teacher/educator, drama coach.
- Sister Mary Regis–Oblate Sisters of Divine Providence; Cathedral School (Charleston, SC); Immaculate Conception HS (Charleston, SC), 50-plus-year educator, administrator.
- Vashti Turley Murphy–Delta Sigma Theta Sorority, Inc. founder, participated in the 1913 Women's Suffrage March; educator, community activist.
- Velma Hopkins–union organizer; civil rights activist.
- Wertie Blackwell Weaver–Delta Sigma Theta Sorority, Inc. founder, participated in the 1913 Women's Suffrage March; educator, author of *The Valley of the Poor*.
- Winona Cargile Alexander–Delta Sigma Theta Sorority, Inc. founder, participated in the 1913 Women's Suffrage March; teacher; first Black female social worker in New York City and the New York County Charities.
- Zephyr Chisom Carter–Delta Sigma Theta Sorority, Inc. founder, participated in the 1913 Women's Suffrage March; educator.

Black Women Leader Activists' Herstories:
An Introduction

I think it is important for African American women to get credit for what we do, and to acknowledge that we are doing it well, and to see ourselves as victorious, and not forget women like (civil rights activist) Fannie Lou Hamer and (newspaper publisher) Ida B. Wells. (Dorothy Height, as cited in Trescott, 1996, p. C1)

Leadership theories have not been readily generalizable to women and *so-called minorities*, in this particular case, African American women. Thus, the result has been "an unfortunate lack of understanding of the importance and role of female" leadership and the networks women create for community leadership (Allen, 1997, p. 61). The *gendered hierarchy* which is divided by race, sexuality, and class explains in part why six women from the late 19th to the late 20th centuries are not found in the traditional discussions of leadership. Walters and Smith (1999) noted that the research that has existed on Black women leaders has featured the neglected role of women activists in the civil rights movement (Crawford, Rouse, & Woods, 1990), interpretative studies on the relative success of African American women leaders (Darcy & Hadley, 1988; Prestage, 1991), and some studies of grassroots or community level Black female leaders (Sack, 1981; Giles, 1988; and Ardey, 1994). For the purposes of this text, an analysis of transformational leadership, critical servant leadership, and social justice leadership found in the exploration of the lives of Fannie Lou Hamer, Septima Clark, Mary McLeod Bethune, Shirley Chisholm, Barbara Jordan, and Audre Lorde seeks not only to chronicle the careers and professional contributions of these women, but also uses these leadership models as units of analysis to highlight their effective leadership *herstories* to inform current practice. For it is important to note that the "powerful and poetic voices" of African American women cannot and should not be ignored or underestimated (Marable, 1998, p. viii).

As African American women who embodied the history, politics, and educational aspirations of an otherwise oppressed people, an analysis of their lived experiences and leadership roles creates a distinctive theoretical and methodological application to leadership theory and practice. These women advance their ideas and theories about leadership through their personal, political, and social activism. Examining these women's lives provides a more complete picture of the effects of race, sexuality, and class and how they are related to current practice in leadership. This inquiry will provide an important (re)visioning of leadership theory by documenting the leadership lives, experiences, and lessons of six strong Black women activists. As Hine and Thompson (1998) made clear and it still rings true today:

> It is tempting to think that Black women are somehow "naturally" stronger and wiser than the rest of the population, that they are born with more courage and resourcefulness and, perhaps, compassion. But that's no more true than any other stereotype. The values that have helped Black women survive are entirely communicable. And at a time when the problems of our society seem insoluble and the obstacles to peace and freedom insurmountable, all Americans have a great deal to learn from the history of Black women in America. (p. 308).

Black women have played and continue to play a pivotal and prominent role in leadership. By contextualizing Black women's experiences as leaders within traditional leadership theories, we are answering the call of scholars (Allen, 1997; Walters & Smith, 1999; Walton, 1994) who beseech the Black academics to theorize and analyze the contributions of Black women within leadership concepts and definitions. Therefore, we heed and answer the clarion call.

Points to Consider

1. How would you define leadership? Is there a one-size-fits-all definition?
2. What are the major differences in the ways in which leadership has been defined throughout time?
3. What is the importance of the historical context as leadership is studied in its current state and in particular as it is viewed through the lens of Black women herstories?
4. Where do Black women fit into the study of leadership? Why is the inclusion of Black women's leadership experiences important?

5. The reality is that there has been race-neutral theorizing (Parker, 2005) in the study of leadership. Discuss and brainstorm solutions to mitigating this issue in leadership.
6. How can the "gendered hierarchy" be flattened so that there is equity for all?
7. Why are "herstories" important in the study of leadership?

Suggested Readings

Alimo-Metcalfe, B., & Alban-Metcalfe, J. (2005). Leadership: Time for a new direction? *Leadership, 1*(1), 51-71.

Alimo-Metcalfe, B. (2010). An investigation of female and male constructs of leadership and empowerment. *Gender in Management: An International Journal, 25*(8), 640-648.

Allen, B. L. (1997). A re-articulation of Black female community leadership: Processes, networks, and a culture of resistance. *African American Research Perspectives, 7*(1), 61-67.

Alston, J. (2005). Tempered radicals and servant leaders: Black females presevering in the superintendency. *Education Administration Quarterly, 41*(4), 675-700.

Anderson, N. (2006). A construct-driven investigation of gender differences in a leadership-role assessment center. *Journal of Applied Psychology, 91*, 555.

Arnot, M. (2002). *Reproducing gender? Essays on educational theory and feminist politics.* London: Routledge/Falmer.

Ashcraft, K. L., & Mumby, D. K. (2004). *Reworking gender: A feminist communicology of organization.* Thousand Oaks, CA: Sage.

Barnett, B. M. (1993). Invisible southern Black women leaders in the civil rights movement: The triple constraints of gender, race, and class. *Gender & Society, 7*(2), 162-182.

Bass, B. M., & Stogdill, R. M. (1990). *Bass and Stogdill's handbook of leadership* (3rd ed.). New York: Free Press.

Billing, Y. D., & Alvesson, M. (2000). Questioning the notion of feminine leadership: A critical perspective on the gender labelling of leadership, gender. *Work and Organization, 7*, 144–57.

Brooks, M. P. & Houck, D. W. (Eds.). (2011). *The speeches of Fannie Lou Hamer.* Jackson, MS: University Press of Mississippi.

Brown, C. S. (Ed.). (1990). *Ready from within, a first person narrative: Septima Clark and the Civil Rights Movement.* Trenton, NJ: Africa World Press, Inc.

Bruckmüller, S., & Branscombe, N. R. (2010). The glass cliff: When and why women are selected as leaders in crisis contexts. *British Journal of Social Psychology, 49*(3), 433-451.

Burns, J. M. (1978). *Leadership.* New York: Harper & Row.

Butler, J. (1990). *Gender trouble: Feminism and the subversion of identity.* London: Routledge

Butterfield,, D. A., & Grinnell, J. P. (1999). "Re-viewing" gender, leadership and managerial behaviour: Do three decades of research tell us anything? Thousand Oaks, CA: Sage.

Christman, D., & Mcclellan, R. (2008). "Living on barbed wire": Resilient women administrators in educational leadership programs. *Educational Administration Quarterly, 44*(1), 3-29.

Ciulla, J. B. (1998). *Ethics, the heart of leadership.* Santa Barbara, CA: Praeger.

Coleman, M. (2003). Gender in educational leadership. In M. Brundrett, N. Burton, & R. Smith (Eds.), *Leadership in education* (pp. 36-51). Thousand Oaks, CA: Sage.

Collier-Thomas, B., & Franklin, V. P. (Eds.). (2001). *Sisters in the struggle: African American women in the civil rights–Black power movement.* New York: New York University Press.

Collins, P. H. (1998). *Fighting words: Black women and the search for justice.* Minneapolis: University of Minnesota Press.

Collins, P. H. (2000). *Black feminist thought: Knowledge, consciousness, and the politics of empowerment* (Vol. 10). New York: Routledge.

Davis, J. (2003). *Learning to lead.* Westport, CT: American Council on Education/Praeger.

Dickerson, N. T. (2006). "We are a force to be reckoned with": Black and Latina women's leadership in the contemporary U.S. labor movement. *WorkingUSA, 9*(3), 293-313.

Drago, E. L. (2006). *Charleston's Avery Center: From education and civil rights to preserving the African American experience.* Charleston, SC: History Press.

Eagly, A. H. (2007). Female leadership advantage and disadvantage: Resolving the contradictions. *Psychology of Women Quarterly, 31*(1), 1-12.

Eagly, A. H., & Carli,, L. L. (2004). *Women and men as leaders.* Thousand Oaks, CA: Sage.

Eagly, A. H., & Johannesen-Schmidt, M. C. (2001). Characteristics of women's leadership: The leadership styles of women and men. *Journal of Social Issues, 57*(4), 781-797.

Elliott, C., & Stead, V. (2008). Learning from leading women's experience: Towards a sociological understanding. *Leadership, 4*(2), 159-180.

Fletcher, J. K. (2004). The paradox of post-heroic leadership: An essay on gender, power, and transformational change. *The Leadership Quarterly, 15*(5), 647-661.

Fiol, M., Harris, D., & House, R. (1999). Charismatic leadership: Strategies for effecting social change. *Leadership Quarterly, 10,* 449-472.

Furst, S. A., & Reeves, M. (2008). Queens of the hill: Creative destruction and the emergence of executive leadership of women. *The Leadership Quarterly, 19*(3), 372-384.

Goleman, D., Boyatzis, R. E., & McKee, A. (2002). *Primal leadership: Realizing the power of emotional intelligence.* Boston, MA: Harvard Business School Press.

Graham, T. S., Sincoff, M. Z., Baker, B. B., & Ackermann, J. C. (2003). Reel leadership: Hollywood takes the leadership challenge http://www.fhsu.edu/jole/issues/JOLE_3_3.pdf

Graham, T. S., Ackermann, J. C., & Maxwell, K. K. (2004). Reel leadership II: Getting emotional at the movies http://www.fhsu.edu/jole/issues/JOLE_3_3.pdf

Grint, K. (2005). Problems, problems, problems: The social construction of "leadership.".*Human Relations, 58,* 1467–94.

Greenleaf, R. K. (1977). *Servant leadership: A journey into the nature of legitimate power and greatness.* New York: Paulist Press.

Groves, K. S. (2005). Gender differences in social and emotional skills and charismatic leadership. *Journal of Leadership & Organizational Studies, 11*(3), 30-46.

Helgesen, S. (1990). *The female advantage: Women's ways of leadership.* New York: Doubleday.

Holvino, E. (2010). Intersections: The simultaneity of race, gender, and class in organization studies. *Gender, Work, and Organization, 17*(3), 248-277.

hooks, b. (1981). *Ain't I a woman: Black women and feminism.* Boston: South End Press.

hooks, b. (1984). *Feminist theory from margin to center.* Boston: South End Press.

hooks, b. (1999). *Ain't I a woman: Black women and feminism.* New York: South End Press.

Horner, M. (1997). Leadership theory: Past, present, & future. *Team Performance Management, 3*(4), 270-287.

House, R. J. (1971). A path-goal theory of leader effectiveness. *Administrative Science Quarterly, 16*, 321-339.

House, R. J. & Mitchell, T. R. (1974). Path-goal theory of leadership. *Journal of Contemporary Business, 3*, 81-97.

Hoyt, C. L. (2005). The role of leadership efficacy and stereotype activation in women's identification with leadership. *Journal of Leadership & Organizational Studies, 11*(4), 2-14.

Indvik, J. (2004). *Women and leadership.* Thousand Oaks, CA: Sage.

James, A. (1998). Mary, Mary quite contrary, How do women leaders grow? *Women in Management Review, 13*, 67-71.

Jean-Marie, G., Williams, V. A., & Sherman, S. L. (2009). Black women's leadership experiences: Examining the intersectionality of race and gender. *Advances in Developing Human Resources, 11*(5), 562-581.

Jogulu, U. D., & Wood, G. J. (2006). The role of leadership theory in raising the profile of women in management. *Equal Opportunities International, 25*(4), 236-250.

Kellerman, B., & Rhode, D. L. (Eds.). (2007). *Women & leadership: The state of play and strategies for change.* San Francisco, CA: John Wiley & Sons.

Kelley, R. E. (1998). In praise of followers. In W. Rosenbach & R. L. Taylor (Eds.), *Contemporary issues in leadership* (4th ed., pp. 96-106). Boulder, CO: Westview.

Klenke, K. (2002). Cinderella stories of women leaders: Connecting leadership contexts and competencies. *Journal of Leadership & Organizational Studies, 9*(2), 18-28.

Klenke, K. (1996). *Women and leadership: A contextual perspective.* New York: Springer.

Kouzes, J. M. & Posner, B. Z. (2008). *The leadership challenge* (4th ed). San Francisco: Jossey-Bass.

Lamsa, A. M., & Sintonen, T. (2001). A discursive approach to understanding women leaders in working life. *Journal of Business Ethics 34,* 255-267.

Lipman-Blumen, J. (2000). *Connective leadership.* Oxford: Oxford University Press.

Lerner, G. (1992). *Black women in White America: A documentary history.* New York: Vintage Books.

Lorenzen, Z. (1996). Female leadership: some personal and professional reflections. *Leadership & Organization Development Journal, 17*(6), 24-31.

Marable, M. (1998). Black leadership: Four great American leaders and the struggle for civil rights. New York: Penguin.

Mathis, R. S. (2007). Relational Leadership: An analysis of The Divine Secrets of the Ya-Ya Sisterhood. *Advances in Developing Human Resources, 9*(2), 199-213.

Meindl, J., Ehrlich, S., & Dukerich, J. (1985). The romance of leadership. *Administrative Science Quarterly, 30,* 78-102.

Morrison, A.M., White, R.P., & Van Velsor, E., & the Center for Creative Leadership. (1992). *Breaking the glass ceiling: Can women reach the top of America's largest corporations* (Upd. ed.). Reading, MA: Addison-Wesley.

Olsson, S. (2000). Acknowledging the female archetype: Women managers' narratives of gender. *Women in Management Review, 15,* 296-302.

Olsson, S. (2002). Gendered heroes: Male and female representations of executive identity. *Women in Management Review, 17,* 142-51.

Ospina, S., & Foldy, E. (2009). A critical review of race and ethnicity in the leadership literature: Surfacing context, power and the collective dimensions of leadership. *The Leadership Quarterly, 20*(6), 876-896.

Parker, P. S. (2005). *Race, gender, and leadership: Re-envisioning organizational leadership from the perspectives of African American women executives.* New Jersey: Lawrence Erlbaum.

Parker, P. S., & Olgivie, D. T. (1996). Gender, culture, and leadership: Toward a culturally distinct model of African-American women executives' leadership strategies. *Leadership Quarterly, 7*(2), 189-214.

Parks, G. S. (2008). *Black Greek letter organizations in the 21st Century: Our fight has just begun.* Lexington, KY: University of Kentucky Press.

Randolph, A. W. (2004). The memories of an all-Black northern urban school: Good memories of leadership, teachers, and the curriculum. *Urban Education, 39*(6), 596-620.

Rosenberg, P. S. (1992). *Race, class and gender in the United States: An integrated study* (2nd ed.). New York: St. Martins Press.

Scott, K. A., & Brown, D. J. (2006). Female first, leader second? Gender bias in the encoding of leadership behavior. *Organizational Behavior and Human Decision Processes, 101*(2), 230-242.

Shamir, B., Dayan-Horesh, H., & Adler, D. (2005). Leading by biography: Towards a life-story approach to the study of leadership. *Leadership, 1*, 13-29.

Sinclair, A. (2005). *Doing leadership differently: Gender, power and sexuality in a changing business culture.* Melbourne: Melbourne University Press.

Stanford, J. H., Oates, B. R., & Flores, D. (1995). Women's leadership styles: A heuristic analysis. *Women in Management Review, 10*, 9-16.

Waring, A. L. (2003). African-American female college presidents: Self conceptions of leadership. *Journal of Leadership & Organizational Studies, 9*(3), 31-44.

West, C., & Zimmerman, D. H. (1987). Doing gender. *Gender and Society, 1*, 125–51.

Western, S. (2008). *Leadership: A critical text.* Los Angeles, CA: Sage.

Wilson, F. (1995). *Organizational behaviour and gender.* London: McGraw-Hill.

van Engen, M., van der Leeden, R., & Willemsen, T. (2001). Gender, context and leadership styles: A field study. *Journal of Occupational and Organizational Psychology, 74*(5), 581-598.

van Emmerik, H., Wendt, H., & Euwema, M. C. (2010). Gender ratio, societal culture, and male and female leadership. *Journal of Occupational and Organizational Psychology, 83*(4), 895-914.

Vroom, V. H. (1964). *Work and motivation.* New York: Wiley.

Walters, R. W. & Smith, R. C. (1999). *African American leadership.* Albany, NY: State University of New York Press.

Yoder, J. D. (2001). Strategies for change: Making leadership work more effectively for women. *Journal of Social Issues, 57*(4), 815-828.

Yukl, G. (2009). *Leadership in organizations* (7th ed.). New York: Prentice Hall.

Video Resources: Teaching/learning tools to be used as supplementary material to support and expand the given topic.

- *A League of Their Own* (1992) – featuring Tom Hanks, Geena Davis, Madonna
- *Joel Barker's Leadershift:* http://www.starthrower.com/joel_barker_leadershift.htm
- *BNET's* Videos: http://www.bnet.com/videos
- *Courage Under Fire* (1996) – featuring Denzel Washington, Meg Ryan, Lou Diamond Phillips
- *Crimson Tide* (1995) – featuring Denzel Washington, Gene Hackman, and Matt Craven
- *Divine Secrets of the Ya-Ya Sisterhood* (2002)–featuring Sandra Bullock, Ellen Burstyn and Fionnula Flanagan
- *Hoosiers* (1986)–featuring Gene Hackman, Dennis Hopper, and Barbara Hershey
- *Norma Rae* (1979)–featuring Sallie Field, Beau Bridges
- Living with Pride: Ruth C. Ellis @ 100 (1999) - featuring Ruth C. Ellis
- *Success Television*: http://www.youtube.com/successtelevision
- The Black Sorority Project: The Exodus (2006)

- *The Contender* (2000) – featuring Jeff Bridges, Gary Oldman, and Joan Allen
- *The Great Escape* (1963) – featuring Steve McQueen, James Garner, and Richard Attenborough
- *The Wall Street Journal* Lessons in Leadership: http://online.wsj.com/public/page/lessons-in-leadership.html
- The Washington Post on Leadership: http://views.washingtonpost.com/leadership/?nid=roll_busin ess

References

Adams, S. (1996). *The Dilbert principle*. New York: HarperCollins.

Adkinson, J. A. (1981). Women in school administration: A review of the research. *Review of Educational Research,51*, 311-343.

Allen, B. L. (1997). A re-articulation of Black female community leadership: Processes, networks, and a culture of resistance. *African American Research Perspectives, 7*(1), 61-67.

Alston, J. (2000). Missing in action: Where are the Black female school superintendents? *Urban Education, 35*(5), 525-531.

Alston, J. (2005). Tempered radicals and servant leaders: Black females presevering in the superintendency. *Education Administration Quarterly, 41*(4), 675-700.

Anderson, M.. (n.d.) Leadership501. Retreived from leadership501.com on December 17, 2010, http://www.leadership501.com/leadership-quotes/316/

Apatheker, B. (1982). *Woman's legacy: Essays on race, sex, and class in American history*. Amherst: The University of Massachusetts Press.

Ardey, S. (1994). The political behavior of Black women: Contextual, structural and psychological factors. In H. Walton (Ed.). *Black politics and Black political behavior*. Westport, CT: Praeger.

Banks, J. (2001). Cultural diversity and education: Foundations, curriculum and teaching, 4th edition. Boston: Allyn and Bacon.

Barnard, C. I. (1938). *The function of the executive*. Cambridge, MA: Harvard University Press.

Barnett, B. M. (1993). Invisible southern Black women leaders in the Civil Rights Movement: The triple constraints of gender, race, and class. *Gender & Society, 7*(2), 162-182.

Bass, B. M., & Stogdill, R. M. (1990). *Bass and Stogdill's handbook of leadership* (3rd ed.). New York: Free Press.

Batten, J. (1989). *Tough-minded leadership.* New York: AMACOM.

Bennis, W. G. (1959). Leadership theory and administrative behavior: The problem of authority. *Administrative Science Quarterly, 4,* 259-260.

Bennis, W. G. (1989). *On Becoming a Leader.* Reading, MA: Addison-Wesley.

Bensimon, E. M., & Neumann, A. (1993). *Redesigning collegiate leadership: Teams and teamwork in higher education.* Baltimore: Johns Hopkins University Press.

Birnbaum, R. (1992). *How academic leadership works: Understanding success and failure in the college presidency.* San Francisco: Jossey-Bass.

Blake, R. R. & McCanse, A. A. (1991). *Leadership dilemmas–Grid solutions.* Houston, TX: Gulf Publishing.

Blake, R. & Mouton, J. (1964). *The managerial grid: The key to leadership excellence.* Houston: Gulf Publishing.

Blanchard, K. (n.d.) Ken Blanchard quotes. Retreived from inspirationalquotes4u.com on December 17, 2010, www.inspirationalquotes4u.com/blanchardquotes/index.html

Blumberg, R. L. (1990). Women in the Civil Rights Movement: Reform or revoultion? *Dialectical Anthropology, 15*(1), 133-139.

Brown, C. S. (Ed.). (1990). *Ready from within, a first person narrative: Septima Clark and the civil rights rovement.* Trenton, NJ: Africa World Press, Inc.

Broverman, I., Vogel, S., Broverman, D., Clarkson, F., & Rosenkrantz, P. S. (1972). Sex-role stereotypes: A current appraisal. *Journal of Social Issues, 28,* 59-78.

Bryman A. (1986). *Leadership and organizations.* London: Routledge and Kegan Paul.

Buchanan, D. & Huczynski, A. (1997). *Organizational behaviour: An introductory text. 3rd ed.* London: Prentice-Hall.

Burns, J. M. (1978). *Leadership.* New York: Harper & Row.

Carter, R.. (n.d.) Leadership quotes. Retreived from buzzle.com on December 17, 2010, http://www.buzzle.com/articles/leadership-quote.html

Chliwniak, L. (1997). *Higher education leadership: Analyzing the gender gap* (ASHE-ERIC Higher Education Report [Vol. 25, No. 4]). Washington, DC: ASHE.

Clark, S. P. (1962). *Echo in my soul.* New York: E. P. Dutton & Co., Inc.

Cohen, W. A. (1990). *The art of a leader.* Englewood Cliffs, NJ: Prentice Hall.

Collier-Thomas, B., & Franklin, V. P. (Eds.). (2001). *Sisters in the struggle: African American women in the civil rights–Black power movement.* New York: New York University Press.

Collins, J. (2001). Good to great: Why some companies make the leap...and others don't. New York: HarperBusiness.

Collins, P. H. (1998). *Fighting words: Black women and the search for justice.* Minneapolis: University of Minnesota Press.

Collins, P. H. (2000). Black feminist thought: Knowledge, consciousness, and the politics of empowerment (Vol. 10). New York: Routledge.

Conger, J. A. (1992). *Learning to lead.* San Francisco: Jossey-Bass.

Covey, S. R. (2000). *The 7 habits of highly effective people.* Philadelphia, PA: Running Press.

Crawford, V. L., Rouse, J. A., & Woods, B. (Eds.). (1993). *Women in the civil rights movement: Trailblazers and torchbearers, 1941-1965.* Bloomington, IN: Indiana University Press.

Cribbin, J. J. (1981). *Leadership: Strategies for organizational effectiveness.* New York: AMACOM.

Darcy, R., & Hadley, C. (1988). Black women in politics: The puzzle of success. *Social Science Quarterly, 69,* 629-645.

Davis, J. (2003). *Learning to lead.* Westport, CT: American Council on Education/Praeger.

Davis, M. (Ed.). (1982). *Contributions of Black women in America* (Vol. 1). Columbia, SC: Kenday Press.

Deaux, K., & Lewis, L. L. (1984). Structure of gender stereotypes: Interrelationships among components and gender. *Journal of Personality and Social Psychology, 46,* 991-1004.

Donelly, J. H., Ivancevich, J. M., & Gibson, J. L. (1985). *Organizations: Behavior, structure, processes* (5th Ed.) Plano, TX: Business Publications Inc.

Doughty, R. (1980). The Black female administrator: Women in a double bind. In S. X. Biklen & M. B. Brannigan (Eds.), *Women and educational leadership* (pp. 165-174). Washington, DC: Lexington Books.

Drath, W. H. & Palus, C. J. (1994). *Making common sense: Leadership as meaning-making in a community of practice.* Greensboro, NC: Center for Creative Leadership.

Drucker, P. E. (2003). *The essential Drucker: The best of sixty years of Peter Drucker's essential writings on management.* New York: Collins Business.

Dupree, M. (n.d.). LeaderValues. Retrieved from leader-values.com on December 17, 2010, http://www.leader-values.com/Content/quotes.asp?Letter=M

Eisenhower, D. D. (n.d.) 25 great quotes on leadership. Retreived from positivityblog.com on December 18, 2010, http://www.positivityblog.com/index.php/2007/07/06/25-great-quotes-on-leadership/l

Fiedler, F. E. (1964). A contingency model of leadership effectiveness. In L. Berkowitz (ed.), *Advances in experimental social psychology*, New York: Academic Press.

Fiedler, F. E. (1967). *A theory of leadership effectiveness*, New York: McGraw-Hill

Firestone, H. (n.d.). LeaderValues. Retrieved from leader-values.com on December 17, 2010, http://www.leader-values.com/Content/quotes.asp?Letter=H

Fleishman, E.A. (1953). Leadership climate and human relations training. *Personnel Psychology, 6*, 205-222.

Fleishman, E. A., Mumford, M. D., Zaccaro, S. J., Levin, K. Y., Korotkin, A. L., & Hein, M. B. (1991). Taxonomic efforts in the description of leader behavior: A synthesis and functional interpretation. *Leadership Quarterly, 2*(4), 245-287.

Flom, E. L. (n.d.) More leadership quotes. Retreived from decision-making-solutions.com on Dec. 18, 2010, http://www.decision-making-solutions.com/leadership_quotes.html

Frasher, J. M., & Frasher, R. S. (1979). Educational administration: A feminine profession. *Educational Administration Quarterly, 2*, 1-13.

Gaines, K. (1996). *Uplifting the race: Black leadership, politics, and culture in the twentieth century.* Chapel Hill, NC: University of North Carolina Press.

Gates, B. (n.d.). 34 awesome quotes on leadership. Retrieved from ideachampion.com on December 17, 2010, http://www.ideachampions.com/weblogs/archives/2010/12/1_management_is.shtml

Giles, C. (1988). Building in many places: Multiple commitments in Black women's community work. In A. Bookman and S. Morgan (Eds.). *Women and the politics of empowerment.* Philadelphia: Temple University Press.

Goleman, D., Boyatzis, R. E., & McKee, A. (2002). *Primal leadership: Realizing the power of emotional intelligence.* Boston, MA: Harvard Business School Press:

Gooden, M. A. (2002). Stewardship and critical leadership: Sufficient for leadership in urban schools? *Education and Urban Society, 35*(1), 133-143.

Greenleaf, R. K. (1977). *Servant leadership: A journey into the nature of legitimate power and greatness.* New York: Paulist Press.

Grimes, M. L. (2005). Re-constructing the leadership model of social justice for African American women in education. *Advancing Women in Leadership Online Journal, 19*(1), 1-6. http://www.advancingwomen.com/awl/fall2005/19_7.html

Handy, C. (1992) The language of leadership. In M. Syrett and C. Hogg (Eds.). *Frontiers of leadership: An essential reader.* Oxford: Blackwell.

Helgesen, S. (1990). *The female advantage: Women's ways of leadership.* New York: Doubleday.

Helgesen, S. (1995). *The web of inclusion: A new architecture for building great organizations.* New York: Currency/Doubleday.

Hemphill, J. K., & Coons, A. E. (1950). *Leadership behavior description.* Columbus, OH: Personnel Research Board, Ohio State University.

Hemphill, J. K., & Coons, A. E. (1957). Development of the leader behavior description questionnaire. In R. M. Stogdill & A. E. Coons (Eds.), *Leader behavior: Its description and measurement* (pp. 147-163, Columbus, OH: Bureau of Business Research, Ohio State University.

Hersey, P., & Blanchard, K. (1986). *Management of organizational behavior.* Englewood Cliffs, NJ: Prentice Hall.

Hill Collins, P. (2008). *Black feminist thought: Knowledge, consciousness, and the politics of empowerment.* New York: Routledge.

Hine, D. C., & Thompson, K. (1998). *A shining thread of hope: The history of Black women in America.* New York: Broadway Books.

Hollander, E. P. (1978). *Leadership dynamics: A practical guide to effective relationships.* New York: Free Press.

Hollander, E. P., & Yoder, J. (1978). *Some issues in comparing women and men as leaders.* (ERIC Document Reproduction Service No. ED 185 883)

Holvino, E. (2010). Intersections: The simultaneity of race, gender, and class in organization studies. *Gender, Work, and Organization, 17*(3), 248-277.

hooks, b. (1981). *Ain't I a woman: Black women and feminism.* Boston: South End Press.

hooks, b. (1984). *Feminist theory from margin to center.* Boston: South End Press.

hooks, b. (1999). *Ain't I a woman: Black women and feminism.* New York: South End Press.

Hooper, G. (n.d.) Leadership quotes. Retreived from ianscotland.com on December 17, 2010, http://www.ianscotland.com/quote_text.htm#Leadership

Horner, M. (1997). Leadership theory: Past, present, & future. *Team Performance Management, 3*(4), 270-287.

Hosking D. M. (1988). Organising, leadership and skillful process. *Journal of Management Studies, 25*, 153

House, R. J. (1971). A path-goal theory of leader effectiveness. *Administrative Science Quarterly, 16*, 321-339.

House, R. J. (1996). Path-goal theory of leadership: Lessons, legacy, and a reformulated theory. *Leadership Theory, 7*(3), 323-352.

House, R. J., & Mitchell, T. R. (1974). Path-goal theory of leadership. *Journal of Contemporary Business, 3,* 81-97.

Huey, J. (1994, February 21). The new post-heroic leadership. *Fortune,* 42-50.

Hull, G. T., & Scott, P. B. (Eds.). (1982). *All the women are white, all the blacks are men: But some of us are brave.* Old Westbury, New York: The Feminist Press.

Jacobs, T. O. & Jaques, E. (1991). Executive leadership. In R. Gal and A. D. Manglesdorff. *Handbook of Military Psychology.* Chichester, England: Wiley.

Janda, K. F. (1960). Towards the explication of the concept of leadership in terms of the concept of power. *Human Relations, 12,* 345-363.

Jaques, E. & Clement, S.D. (1994). *Executive leadership: A practical guide to managing complexity.* Cambridge, MA: Carson-Hall & Co. Publishers

Jean-Marie, G., Williams, V. A., & Sherman, S. L. (2009). Black women's leadership experiences: Examining the intersectionality of race and gender. *Advances in Developing Human Resources, 11*(5), 562-581.

Katz D., & Kahn, R. L. (1978). *The social psychology of organizations.* New York: Wiley.

Kellerman, B., & Rhode, D. L. (Eds.). (2007). *Women & leadership: The state of play and strategies for change.* San Francisco, CA: John Wiley & Sons.

Kelley, R. E. (1998). In praise of followers. In W. Rosenbach & R. L. Taylor (Eds.), *Contemporary issues in leadership* (4th ed., pp. 96-106). Boulder, CO: Westview.

Kennedy, J. F. (n.d.) 25 great quotes on leadership. Retrieved from positivityblog.com on December 18, 2010, http://www.positivityblog.com/index.php/2007/07/06/25-great-quotes-on-leadership/l

Klenke, K. (1996). *Women and leadership: A contextual perspective.* New York: Springer.

Korah, S. (1990). Multiculturalism and the woman of colour: Can we bridge the gap between rhetoric and reality? *Tiger Lily: Journal of Women of Colour, 5,* 5-20.

Kouzes, J. M. & Posner, B. Z. (1995). *The leadership challenge* (1st ed.). San Francisco: Jossey-Bass.

Lamsa, A.-M., & Sintonen, T. (2001) A discursive approach to understanding women leaders in working life. *Journal of Business Ethics, 34,* 255-267.

Lee, C. K. (2000). *For freedom's sake: The life of Fannie Lou Hamer.* Chicago: University of Illinois Press.

Lewin, K., Lippitt, R., & White, R. K. (1939). Patterns of aggressive behavior in experimentally created "social constructs." *Journal of Science Psychology, 10,* 271-299.

Likert, R. (1958). Effective supervision: An adaptive and relative process.*Personnel Psychology, 11*(3), 317-332.

Likert, R. (1961). *New patterns of management.* New York: McGraw Hill.

Lippman, W. (n.d.) Leadership quotes. Retrieved from buzzle.com on December 17, 2010, http://www.buzzle.com/articles/leadership-quotes.html

Marable, M. (1998). *Black leadership: Four great American leaders and the struggle for civil rights.* New York: Penguin.

Martin, P. Y. (1996) Gendering and evaluating dynamics: Men, masculinities and managements. In D. L. Collinson & J. Hearn (Eds.). *Men as managers. Managers as men: Critical perspectives on men, masculinities and managements,* (pp. 186-209). London: SAGE.

Maxwell, J. (1998). *21 irrefutable laws of leadership: Follow them and people will follow you.* Nashville, TN: Thomas Nelson.

Montgomery, F. M. (n.d.). Definitions. Retrieved from thepracticeofleadership.net on December 18, 2010, http://www.thepracticeofleadership.net/tag/definitions/

Nader, R. (n.d.) Ralph Nader quotes. Retreived from thinkexist.com on December 17, 2010, http://thinkexist.com/quotation/the_function_of_leadership_is_t o_produce_more/224785.html

Nkomo, S. M. (1992). The emperor has no clothes: Rewriting "race in organizations." *Academy of Management Review, 17*(3), 487-513.

Norton, M. S. (2005) *Executive leadership for effective administration.* Boston: Pearson.

Ortiz, F. I. (1982). *Career patterns in education: Men, women and minorities in public school administration.* New York: Praeger.

Payne, C. M. (1995). I've got the light of freedom: The organizing tradition and the Mississippi freedom struggle. Berkeley, CA: University of California Press.

Parker, P. S. (2005). *Race, gender, and leadership: Re-envisioning organizational leadership from the perspectives of African American women executives.* New Jersey: Lawrence Erlbaum.

Parker, P. S., & Olgivie, D. T. (1996). Gender, culture, and leadership: Toward a culturally distinct model of African-American women executives' leadership strategies. *Leadership Quarterly, 7*(2), 189-214.

Patton, G. S. (n.d.). LeaderValues.
Retrieved from leader-values.com on December 17, 2010, http://www.leader-values.com/Content/quotes.asp?Letter=G

Peters, T. J., & Waterman, R. H. Jr. (1984). *In search of excellence: Lessons from America's best run companies.* New York: Warner Books.

Peterson, M. (1997). Using contextual planning to transform institutions. In M. Peterson, D. Dill, L. A. Mets, & Associates (Eds.), *Planning and management for a changing environment.* (pp. 127-157). San Francisco: Jossey-Bass.

Prentice, W. C. H. (1961). Understanding leadership. *Harvard Business Review, 39*(5), 143-151.

Rauch, C. F., & Behling, O. (1984). Functionalism: Basis for alternate approach to the study of leadership. In J.G. Hunt, D. M. Hosking, C. A Schriesheim and R. Stewart (Eds.). *Leaders and managers: International perspectives on managerial behavior and leadership* (pp. 45-62). Elmsford, New York: Pergamon Press,

Richards, D., & Engel, S. (1986). After the vision: Suggests to corporate visionaries and vision champions. In Adams, J. D. (Ed.), *Transforming leadership,*(pp. 199-215). Alexandria, VA: Miles River Press,

Robnett, B. (1996). African American women in the Civil Rights Movement, 1954-1965: Gender, leadership, and microbilization. *American Journal of Sociology, 101*(6), 1661-1693.

Robnett, B. (1997). How long? How long? African American women in the struggle for civil rights. New York: Oxford University Press.

Rost, J. C. (1991). *Leadership for the twenty-first century.* New York: Praeger.

Rost, J. C. (1993). *Leadership for the twenty-first century.* New York: Praeger.

Rusher, A. W. (1996). *African American women administrators.* Lanham, MD: University Press of America.

Sack, K. (1988). Gender and grassroots leadership. In A. Bookman and S. Morgan (Eds.). *Women and the politics of empowerment.* Philadelphia: Temple University Press.

Schein, E. (1992). *Organizational culture and leadership.* San Francisco: Jossey-Bass.

Schwarzkopf, H. N. (n.d.). Leadership quotes. Retrieved from buzzle.com on December 17, 2010, http://www.buzzle.com/articles/leadership-quotes.html

Senge, P. M. (1990). The fifth discipline: The art and practice of the learning organization. New York: Doubleday/Currency.

Senge, P. M. (1994). *The fifth discipline.* New York: Doubleday/Currency.

Shakeshaft, C. S. (1985). Strategies for overcoming the barriers to women in educational administration. In S. Klein (Ed.), *Handbook for achieving sex equity through education* (pp. 124-144). Baltimore, MD: The Johns Hopkins University Press.

Smircich, L. & Stubbart, C. (1982). Strategic management in an enacted world. *Academy of Management Review, 10,* 724-736.

Stogdill, R. H. (1950). Leadership, membership *and* organization. *Psychological Bulletin, 47,* 1-14.

Stogdill, R. H. (1974). *Handbook of leadership: A survey of theory and research.* New York: The Free Press.

Stogdill, R. H. (1981). Traits of leadership: A follow-up to 1970. In B. Bass (Ed.), *Handbook of leadership.* New York: The Free Press.

Stogdill, R. M. & Coons, A. E. (1957). *Leader behavior: Its description and measurement.* Columbus, OH: Bureau of Business Research, The Ohio State University.

Tannenbaum, R., Weschler, I. R., and Massarik, F. (1961). *Leadership and organization: A behavioral approach.* New York: McGraw-Hill.

Tate IV, W. F. (1997). Critical race theory and education: History, theory, and implications. *Review of Research in Education, 22,* 195-247.

Townsend, B. K., & Twombly, S. B. (1998). A feminist critique of organizational change in the community college. In. J. S. Levin (Ed.), *Organizational change in the community college: A ripple or a sea change?* (pp. 77-85). San Francisco: Jossey-Bass.

Tozer, J. (n.d.) Leadership quotes.
Retrieved from strategicleadership.com on December 17, 2010, http://www.strategicleadership.com.au/Strategic_Leadership_P ty_Ltd/Quotations. html

Trescott, J. (1996, September 8). An affirmative action: Black women's group invests in its future. *The Washington Post,* p. C1.

Tzu, L. (n.d.) Lao Tzu biography.
Retrieved from biographybase.com on December 17, 2010, http://www.biographybase.com/biography/Lao_Tzu.html

Vecchio, R. (1988). Situational leadership theory: An examination of a prescriptive theory. *Journal of Applied Psychology, 72,* 444-451.

Wacjman, J. (1998) *Managing like a man. Women and men in corporate life.* Cambridge: Polity Press.

Walters, R. W., & Smith, R. C. (1999). *African American leadership.* Albany, NY: State University of New York Press.

Walton, H. (Ed.). (1994). *Black politics and Black political behavior: A linkage analysis.* Santa Barbara, CA: Greenwood Publishing Group.

Washington, J. (Ed.). (1992). *A testament of hope: The essential writings of Martin Luther King, Jr.* New York: Harper Row.

Weber, M. (1947). *The theory of social and economic organization.* Translated by A. M. Henderson & Talcott Parsons. New York: The Free Press.

Webber, A. M. (1996, June 30). Destiny as the job of the leader. Retrieved from http://www.fastcompany.com/magazin/03 jaworski.html

Wilson, M. (2004). Closing the leadership gap: Why women can and must help run the world. New York: Penguin.

Yukl, G. (2009). *Leadership in organizations* (7th ed.). New York: Prentice Hall.

Zaleznik, A. (1992). Managers and leaders: Are they different? *Harvard Business Review, 70*(2), *126*-135.

Zander, B. (2001). *Leadership: The art of possibility* [DVD]. http://www.videoarts.com/product/ZAN1/Leadership:-an-art-of-possibility

Critical Servant Leadership: The Gift of Leadership and the Burden of Sacrifice

Even in pre-civil war days, Black women stood in the vanguard for equal rights; for freedom from slavery, for recognition of women as citizens and co-partners with men in all of life's endeavors...However, because of the nature of American history, and particularly because of institutions of slavery and segregation, the names and lives of Black women leaders are all but unknown in American society.–Margaret Walker (Sterling, 1979 as cited in Barnett 1993, p.163)

Ironically, Dr. Walker's words ring true 31 years later. This statement is thought provoking in that it conveys how far American society as well as the American educational system has come in terms of the leadership knowledge of Black women. The achievements of Black women have not been celebrated, recorded, or deemed important enough to be included in the canon of leadership and organizational studies (Hine & Thompson, 1998; Holvino, 2010; Parker, 2005; Parker & Olgivie, 1996). However, scholars such as Hine and Thompson (1998), Parker (1996, 2005), Alston (2000, 2005), hooks (1981, 1984) and others (see Barnett, 1993; Collier-Thomas & Franklin, 2001; Collins, 2000, 2004; Hull & Scott, 1982; Murtadha-Watts, 1999) are committed to documenting and preserving the legacy of Black women leaders. Within the tradition of preserving the legacy of Black women leaders, this chapter adds another dimension by focusing on critical servant leadership (McClellan, 2006, 2010) as a unit of analysis to discuss the lives of Fannie Lou Hamer and Septima Poinsette Clark.

The idea of respecting and learning from the historical plight of Black women leaders as a source of valuable knowledge may be seen as counterproductive in a society that has systemically devalued the contributions of Black women (Collins, 1998; A. Y. Davis, 1981; M. Davis, 1982). Throughout history and in popular culture, Black women have been degraded as hypersexual women, mammies, the welfare queen, and the masculine matriarch of the Black family (Collins, 1996; Lubiano, 1992; Walker, 1983). Black women were all too aware of the images that were designed to destroy and devalue their contributions to the Black community as well as society in general. In 1851, Sojourner Truth said it best: Ain't I a woman?, referencing the harsh reality of Black women's lives during slavery as a field hand, a mother with no rights to her children, a woman deemed unworthy to gentlemanly courtesy, and a woman defenseless against sexual violation from her master. Even though these images translated into harsh realities in the daily lives of Black women from slavery through the 1960's, Black women relied on a spiritual resistance of oratorical prowess, self-determination and empowerment, and building community to combat the racist patriarchal discourses, policies, and laws to improve the quality of Black life.

By revisiting the lives of Fannie Lou Hamer and Septima Poinsette Clark, through the lens of critical servant leadership (McClellan, 2006, 2010), the role spirited resistance played in their leadership becomes more apparent. The remainder of the chapter will define as well as critique contemporary notions of servant leadership, highlight leadership lives of Hamer and Clark, and conclude with a discussion on the exclusion of Black women's leadership voice from the leadership and organizational studies canon.

Black Women Leaders in the Civil Rights Movement: Invisible, Yet Indispensable

In spite of the performance of highly valuable roles in the civil rights movement, Black women such as Septima Clark, Fannie Lou Hamer, Ella Baker, Dorothy Cotton, Daisy Bates, and Diane

Nash, just to name a few, remain a class of unsung heroes (Barnett, 1993) and underresearched leaders. While navigating their role as Black women in a racist patriarchal society, these women were more than followers in the civil rights movement. They were leaders who performed a variety of roles comparable to those of Black men (1993). Due to constraining forces at the time, these women were seldom recognized as leaders, although they were often the ones who initiated protests, formulated strategies and tactics as well as mobilized resources through fundraising, aligned personnel, and developed communication networks and organizations to disseminate information for collective action and civil disobedience (Barnett, 1993; Collier-Thomas & Franklin, 2001; Crawford, Rouse, & Woods, 1993). For example, as far back as 1895, the National Association of Colored Women (NACW) was established by the merger of the National Federation of Afro-American women and National League of Colored Women of Washington, DC (Parker, 2005). Founders of NACW include Harriet Tubman, Ida B. Wells, and Mary Church Terrell. The NACW became involved in campaigns in favor of women's suffrage, against lynching and Jim Crow laws, as well as led efforts to improve education. Ironically, the motto of the NACW was "lifting as we climb."

The Montgomery Bus Boycott propelled Dr. King into national prominence as a leader. However, JoAnn Robinson, an English professor at Alabama State University and other educated women of the Women's Political Council (WPC) organized and planned the boycott (Barnett, 1993). They disseminated information about the boycott and distributed approximately 35,000 leaflets following the arrest of Rosa Parks. With as much tenacity and commitment, Georgia Gilmore, a cook and domestic worker performed another important role in the boycott (Barnett, 1993). She single handedly organized the Club from Nowhere, which she named to avoid compromising White as well as Black donors to support the boycott (Barnett, 1993). In doing so, she along with many others was fired from her job; educated and non-educated alike. Herein are merely two examples among many of the leadership resistance led by Black women

Hindsight can be 20/20. Today, a majority of these women are referred to as leaders, but in the midst of resistance and protest, they were sisters in struggle united by a collective vision of self-determination, empowerment, and justice for the Black community. Their backgrounds spanned class distinctions and educational attainment. They yearned to increase the quality of life of Blacks in education, health care, and civil rights. They fought for civil rights at a time when state-sanctioned violence was the norm and death was imminent. Black women fought alongside Black men for civil rights and bore the burden of the same harsh punishment (loss of income, beatings, jail, rape, and death) for violating Jim Crow and the White man's system of order in the South.

Patriarchy shaped the lives of Black women and had a drastic hold on the roles women were relegated to during the civil rights movement. Nevertheless, women performed roles that in present eyes would deem them heroes of the movement (Barnett, 1993; Robnett, 1997). However, as scholars (Collier-Thomas & Franklin, 2001; Crawford, et al., 1993; Hine, 1993; Hine & Thompson, 1998) have documented, this class of women remain unsung heroes of American history. The constraining forces maintaining the invisibility of this class of women leaders are the result of sexism, racism, and classism that were customary in the movement (Lawson & Payne, 1998; Payne, 1995) and are prevalent in leadership literature (Holvino, 2010; Parker, 2005) and feminist scholarship (Collins, 1996, 1998, 2000; hooks, 1981, 1984). A majority of the civil rights movement scholarship has centered on the "great men" leaders by focusing on their charisma or leading roles via their position, White women activists, or benevolent elite supporters of the movement who donated money to the cause (Hull & Scott, 1982; Jenkins & Eckert, 1986). The exclusion of Black women's roles in leadership literature and the overusage of the "great man" leadership analysis limits our understanding of leadership as practiced by Black women activists. For the sake of adding to the knowledge gap on Black women's leadership praxis, servant leadership and critical servant leadership are used as a leadership analysis in the lives of Fannie Lou Hamer and Septima Poinsette Clark.

Critical Servant Leadership: A Spirited Resistance Defined

Critical servant leadership is a theoretical construct originated from a research study on servant leadership and spiritual practices of Black leaders using portraiture as the qualitative methodology (McClellan, 2006). Critical servant leadership is an expansion of servant leadership by combining it with critical spirituality (Dantley, 2003). In the following sections, critical spirituality is defined, servant leadership is defined and critiqued, and critical servant leadership is discussed within the context of Black women's leadership.

Servant Leadership Defined

The term *servant leadership* was coined by Robert K. Greenleaf in his seminal essay "The Servant as Leader" (1977). In it, he defines servant leadership as a way to serve and lead as a way of expanding service to individuals and institutions. Servant leadership or leadership as service is germane to those who fought for civil rights and social justice. Black women such as those previously mentioned were almost always preoccupied with building community through their service and activism. Greenleaf may have coined the term servant leadership, but Black women leaders throughout history have mastered the application and implementation of servant leadership.

The key elements of servant leadership are to encourage collaboration, trust, foresight, and provide the foundation of the ethical use of power (Spears, 1995) via a leadership role. In theory, servant leadership thrives on the concept of reciprocity. In this regard, the job of the servant as leader is to enlist others in an effort to build a community of practice that motivates members to create shared knowledge and shared ways of knowing (Drath & Palus, 1994). This type of leader is committed to serving others through a cause, a crusade, a movement, and a campaign with humanitarian, not materialistic, goals (Williams, 1998).

Typically the servant leader possesses a charismatic, persuasive personality that inspires confidence, helping others to weather the storms of doubt and despair that inevitably arise in emotionally laden circumstances in which ideology and action lines are drawn (Williams, 1998). The servant leader eschewing opportunistic motives of personal gain and self-aggrandizement is willing to take risks to achieve a higher good. These risks are hefty, time consuming, and often times life altering. Black women lost their jobs for registering to vote, passing out leaflets, and refusing to rescind membership in organizations such as the NAACP. Fannie Lou Hamer and Septima Clark are such women who endured these hardships. At times, the servant leader must be willing to lead in the face of danger and extreme adversity (Williams, 1998). As documented, Black women faced danger alongside men. In this regard, they were more vulnerable due to the threat of sexual violation and rape. Nevertheless, she is guided by an overarching, prophetic, transforming vision that is carefully conceived and simply articulated (Williams, 1998). Similar to the tenets as described by Dantley's (2003) critical spirituality, servant leadership is not only about "doing" the acts of service, but also "being" a steward, entrusted with responsibility, and accountable to a larger community. By precept and example, a servant leader is to co-create a shared vision, sharing learned knowledge, and building upon the skills and abilities that foster co-creating of processes that sustain the vision.

The servant model of leadership has nine functional attributes (vision, honesty, integrity, trust, service, modeling, pioneering, appreciation of others, and empowerment) (Russell & Stone, 2002) and 11 accompanying attributes (communication, credibility, competence, stewardship, visibility, influence, listening, encouragement, teaching, and delegation), which provide direction for practical implementation (p. 153). Servant leadership as a researchable and applicable leadership phenomenon is scarce in that the very notion of *servant leader* may appear to be an oxymoron (Sendjaya & Sarros, 2002). To some, it may be difficult to think and act as a leader and servant at the same time. Nevertheless, for women such as Fannie Lou Hamer and Septima Poinsette Clark, the relationships between service and leadership are compatible and intertwined (Clark, 1962, 1986; Collier-Thomas & Franklin, 2001; Crawford, 2001; Lee, 2000, 2001; Payne, 1995).

Servant Leadership Critiqued

Servant leadership in its current theoretical positioning in the academy and organized social spaces is touted as the next wave of revolutionary thinking (Eicher-Catt, 2005) which is noteworthy. However, the range of scholars and practitioners that define, study, and teach about servant leadership are from business-oriented disciplines that inadvertently serve the needs of big business and the managerial elite. This coincidence noted by feminist scholars such as Eicher-Catt (2005) and Nadesan (1999) infers that the servant leadership discourse has taken the form of *evangelical capitalism* in an effort to mend the contradictions of public service and commerce and serve political as well as financial ends of corporate elite. Servant leadership as couched in many higher education institutions promotes a genderless, colorblind, and deficient social justice orientation of leadership. Yet, a genderless, colorblind, and deficient social justice orientation of leadership is impossible given that the historical inferences to its implementation and application are examples of leadership focused on social justice activism. Historically, American institutions are grounded in hegemonic practices that benefit White male leadership ideals over those of any raced and gendered group that deviates from the status quo. Insidiously, servant leadership theory in its current form as taught and researched perpetuates a long standing masculine-feminine and master-slave dichotomy as well as promotes a White evangelical conservative political economy that in the end contradicts the revolutionary potential of servant leadership (Eicher-Catt, 2005). In addition, servant leadership discourse as currently positioned seems euphoric. The discourse lacks a zealousness and urgency on how to use and apply servant leadership in extreme situations.

This elitist perspective of mainstream servant leadership perpetuates the exclusionary models of top-down pyramidal leadership, negating the energy derived from a broader, more inclusive base of decision making and planning (Childs, 1989).

The least privileged should benefit from servant leadership. Greenleaf (1977) argued that individual actions are responsible for the good and evil in the world. And, these actions have manifested in America's most prized institutions. Therefore, it is pertinent to expand the servant leadership discourse to move beyond the current preoccupation with a genderless, colorblind, and deficient social justice model of servant leadership. This notion of servant leadership has been promoted and co-opted into something that it's not supposed to be. Servant leadership specifically deals with socially just ideals of helping the least privileged in society, but this is not communicated by those who espouse to be the preeminent scholars and practitioners of servant leadership. Leaders such as Fannie Lou Hamer and Septima Poinsette Clark exemplify servant leadership in a critical context that combats the status quo and fought for what was right, fair, and moral.

Servant Leadership Expanded

The current state of servant leadership discourse is stagnant and pays minimal attention to community transformation, educational equality, economic development, and/or political enfranchisement. Servant leadership scholars need to analyze what is taught, researched, and practiced as leadership and begin to examine the complexities and challenges that faced past servant leaders and aspirant servant leaders. Therefore, critical servant leadership is offered as an expansion of the co-opted version of servant leadership in an effort to cross-examine the lives of historical leaders, to be inclusive of the spiritual foundation leaders, and to promote a discourse that incorporates the context of the social space in which leadership was applied.

Critical servant leadership is a framework that originated from a research study on servant leadership and the spiritual practices that influenced their leadership (McClellan, 2006, 2010). Critical servant leadership is birthed from a perspective grounded in the African American experience. In this regard, critical servant leadership is an amalgamation of critical spirituality (Dantley, 2003) and servant leadership (Greenleaf, 1977; Williams, 1998). Critical spirituality is the by-product of the infusion of two radical perspectives, which are critical theory and Cornel West's notion of prophetic spirituality. Critical spirituality has three major components. The first component is a prophetic spirituality, which is a combative spirituality and frames the urgency for institutional and personal transformation. The second component is the impact of reflection on the leader(s). The third and final component is a spirit filled resistance that proposes a project or praxis for self and institutional change. The overarching goal of critical spirituality is to critique and destroy undemocratic power relations blended with a spiritual reflection grounded in an African American sense of moralism and prophetic resistance (Dantley, 2003). In this vein, critical spirituality coupled with a servant leadership orientation provides us with a new unit of analysis to examine the leadership practices of exemplary leaders such as Fannie Lou Hamer and Septima Poinsette Clark.

Critical servant leadership, an extension of servant leadership and critical spirituality, is all encompassing of the underlying foundations of servant leadership and the overarching goal of critical spirituality. In this regard, critical servant leadership is more than a leadership theory; it is a way of being, a connection to communities and people who are marginalized, frowned upon, and separated by the mainstreams of society. A critical servant leader is guided by a willingness and commitment to promote and sustain equity, fairness, and social justice. One merely does not practice critical servant leadership; one is a critical servant leader (McClellan, 2010). The critical servant leader's way of being is based on their worldview and has the capacity for reciprocity. Next, the leadership of Fannie Lou Hamer and Septima Poinsette Clark will be explored through the lens of critical servant leadership.

Herstory–Fannie Lou Hamer:
The Conscience of the Civil Rights Movement

Fannie Lou Townsend was born on a plantation in Montgomery County, Mississippi in 1917. She was the last of 20 children born to Jim and Lou Ella Townsend and lived what some of us would call a horrendous life. She was born into abject poverty and a highly racial, hostile, and terror-filled environment. She'd been working the cotton fields since she was six years old. She yearned for a better life as she knew all too well the backbreaking work of picking cotton accompanied with the lack of reward and compensation that followed. But at the middle age of 42, Fannie Lou Hamer found her voice, longed for liberation from the oppressive policies of racist Mississippi, and became a servant of the people (Williams, 1998).

Disappointed but Not Deterred

On August 27, 1962, the Student Nonviolent Coordinating Committee (SNCC) visited Ruleville, Mississippi, the residence of Fannie Lou Hamer, for a mass meeting on voter registration. SNCC educated the locals about their civil rights and the process for voter registration. SNCC knew that choosing Hamer was key as Miles (1993) noted:

> Fannie Lou had a presence. She was smart. And as a poor Black southern sharecropper, she represented the soul of the people whom the movement wanted to represent. As disenfranchised people were starting to assert themselves, she stepped forward, voicing her own concerns and those of her neighbors. She had a personal story, which would only grow more compelling the more she endured. And she had a voice with which to tell it. Virtually everyone whose path crossed hers remembered first and foremost her singing and her speaking. (p. 41)

Hamer, 42 years old, already sensed that change was on the horizon and decided to be among those citizens that would take the bus ride to the city of Indianola to take the literacy test to vote. Working with SNCC, they became known as the "Indianola 18"

(Lee, 2000; Mills, 1993). This decision was undoubtedly influenced by the excitement she felt at the possibility of realizing a better life–a life defined by something more than suffering and neglect (Lee, 2001; Mills, 1993). Reflecting on that moment, Hamer said:

> I could just see myself voting people outta office that I know was wrong and didn't do nothing to help the poor. I said, you know, that's sumpin' I really wanna be involved in, and finally at the end of that rally, I had made up my mind that I was gonna come out there when they said you could go down that Friday to try to register (Raines, 1977, p. 249)

Not only was Hamer the first to commit to go vote, but through an unplanned and inspirational speech, she encouraged others to make the choice as well. From then on, she began taking initiatives to promote collective struggle for real power (Lee, 2001). Although Hamer traveled to Indianola, she flunked the literacy test the first time, but passed on the third try after taking citizenship classes as Highlander Folk School, which were often taught by Septima Poinsette Clark. Voting out the people in office who despised the poor Black Mississippians was at her fingertips, but failed to happen immediately because she did not have the two-thirds property tax receipts required by Mississippi law at the time. This experience was what Hamer called an "ordeal" (Mills, 1993, p. 142). However, she realized the strength in numbers as an identifiable group of people who were bound by common concerns and committed to achieving basic civil rights.

Not all were pleased with Hamer's decision to exercise her civil rights to vote. Hamer lived on a plantation that was owned by W. D. Marlow, where she and her family were sharecroppers. Marlow demanded that she return to the courthouse and rescind her voter application. In Hamer's recollection of the incident, Marlow said:

> Well I mean that you going to have to tell me whether you going back and withdraw your registration or you going to have to leave here. We're not going to have this in Mississippi, and you will have to withdraw. I am looking for your answer, yea or nay? I'll give you until tomorrow morning. And if you don't withdraw you will have to leave. (Mills, 1993, p. 145)

Hamer was disappointed in Marlow's reaction. She was livid
and more importantly insulted that he would be so unappreciative
and selfish. She expected some decency; after all, she showed care
and concern for him and his family. She reflected and said:

> I just thought to myself, "what does he really care about us?" I had been
> workin' there for eighteen years. I had baked cakes and sent them
> overseas to him during war. I had nursed his family, cleaned his house,
> stayed with his kids. I had handled his time book and his payroll. Yet he
> wanted me out. I made up my mind I was grown and I was tired.
> (Edgerton, 1970, pp. 97-98)

Her decision not to rescind her registration resulted in her
eviction. She stated in response, "I didn't go down there to register
for you. I went to register for myself" (Edgerton, 1970, pp. 97-98).
That night with the help of some of the SNCC volunteers, she
moved out, leaving home and family for the freedom to act on her
own behalf. According to Marlow, Fannie Lou's husband still had a
debt of $300, so he had to stay to work off the debt. A year later he
was fired. The risks a servant leader endures are immense and life
altering. This example of Fannie Lou Hamer being evicted for
voting demonstrates that servant leadership is not only about
doing the acts of service, but also *being* a servant and being
entrusted with the responsibility of demanding economic,
educational, and/or political changes that transform communities
and institutions for generations.

Hamer wholeheartedly believed that poor Black Mississippians
should benefit from her work as a leader in the community. She
promoted a political agenda that addressed their needs for equal
education, better health care, and political enfranchisement
through voter registration. She was impatient and angry at the
conditions in Mississippi. In her speeches and daily organizing,
she transformed her anger into formidable personal power. Hamer
understood and articulated the yearnings of poor Mississippians
and knew their unspoken fears (Williams, 1998). Hamer's example
of endurance emboldened and uplifted a community's
determination to tackle and overcome the repression and terror
associated with racism in Mississippi.

"I am sick and tired of being sick and tired": Injustice No More

While political enfranchisement was her longest running battle and under girded all that she did, it was not the only crusade Hamer waged. Wherever she went, Hamer talked about the condition of Black Mississippians, the grinding poverty, economic deprivation, inadequate education, and poor health care (Lee, 2000, 2001; Mills, 1993). Mrs. Hamer was infuriated at the education system in Mississippi, especially the way Black boys and girls were portrayed in the few books they had to read. In a reflection of her experiences in public school, she said:

> When I was in public school, the state of Mississippi was responsible for doing a very sad thing. When I was in school, it must have been in a child's third reader. I read about a little child and this little child was Black and his name was Epamonandus. First place, it was stupid to put a word that big in a book for a kid. Second place, it was a disgrace the way they had this little child and the things that he was doing. The child was portrayed as stupid, as were his mother and grandmother. (Mills, 1993, p. 13)

As she became more involved in civil rights activism, Hamer spoke more freely about injustices in the health care system as well. In 1961, Hamer was sterilized without her knowledge or permission. She went into the hospital to have a small uterine cyst removed, but was given a hysterectomy. As she was recuperating, she heard what they were talking about in the big house on the plantation. Passing conversations through Vera Alice Wallace, cousin of the doctor and wife of the plantation owner, spread the word that Hamer's uterus was removed. How devastating to have your choice of child bearing being stripped without consent. Years later, a similar case of two sisters who were sterilized at an Alabama family planning clinic was in the national news. Their mother, who was illiterate, signed a form that she didn't understand. She thought they were receiving anti-fertility shots, but their uteruses were removed. Hamer had been telling her story for years. There was no way she would even consider suing. In her own words, "Getting a white lawyer to go against a white doctor. I would have been taking my hands and screwing tacks in my own casket" (Young, 1976).

Hamer summoned personal memory to create a larger context and meaning for a contemporary political movement. For her, struggle was historical and continuous. She used survival of personal tragedy to instill others with a sense of outrage and an abiding commitment to do anything to make significant changes. Hamer's shared trials and tribulations nurtured the bonds of trust between her and the community she served (Williams, 1998). This was critically important given the risks of personal safety involved in her giving voice to the problems, while employing civil disobedience tactics as she fought for civil rights. Her legitimacy was rooted in her authenticity and proximity to her community, not solely on her ability to bridge formal leaders and organizations with the masses (Lee, 2000, 2001). Ending human suffering was a political obsession for Hamer and this included suffering caused by decades of poverty and lack of education. She was called by many a *straight shooter*. She cut to the heart of an issue with passion, integrity, and undying truth. Eleanor Holmes Norton (current DC delegate to the U. S. House of Representatives), a law student at the time who tried to get Hamer out of jail in Winona (also the jail where she experienced the horrific beating) for trying to vote described her in this way:

> The capacity to put together a mosaic of coherent thought about freedom and justice so that when it was all through, you knew what you had heard because it held together with wonderful cohesion. Her speeches and themes, they had lessons. They had principles. And then when you had heard all that said with such extraordinary brilliance, like WOW, that's what it is. She has put her finger on something truly important that all of us felt, but she had said. You heard that all the time. What really gets you is that person somehow concretizes an idea that you had never quite been able to fully form. And she did that in this extraordinary ringing style and then ended up singing "this little light of mine." You never needed to hear anybody else speak again (Mills, 1993, p. 85)

If it were up to Fannie Lou Hamer, "the poor would and should have a voice in their own destiny through meaning franchise" (Lee,

2000; Mills, 1993, p. 164). Motivated by the unconquerable desire of the human spirit to be free, servant leaders such as Fannie Lou Hamer emerged, willing to endure strife, deprivation, terror and possibly death that waited. She became an example of a towering moral and political force throughout the south (Mills, 1993).

Spiritual Resilience: Faith Is My Shield

For Fannie Lou Hamer, civil rights activism was a natural expression her spirituality in practice. She was widely known for quoting the Bible frequently in her challenges to White supremacy and appealed to the moral conscience of White Americans (Crawford, 2001). In one of her many speeches before a mass civil rights meeting, she warned how the continuation of racism threatened the moral fabric of American society. Hamer was not only a powerful orator, but her singing also inspired many civil rights meetings. One activist recalled that when "Mrs. Hamer finishes singing a few freedom songs, one is aware that he has truly heard a fine political speech, stripped of the usual rhetoric and filled with the anger and spirit filled determination of the civil rights movement" (Crawford, 2001; Spencer, 1987 as cited in Crawford, 2001). She embraced *moral pragmatism* as a spiritually based political perspective. The most pressing community needs determined her political agenda. Hamer's moral pragmatist approach was based on her sense of community allegiance and Christian obligation (Lee, 2001).

When leading a cause, such as civil rights and helping the least privileged in society, the ultimate goal can seem elusive and doubtful at times. Yet, the servant leader, with a critical orientation is sustained by and draws from an abiding faith–faith in God, faith in self and others, faith in the vision and integrity of the cause. Hamer almost always alluded to her faith and how that was a sustaining power in her life (Williams, 1998). Faith played a defining role in Hamer's leadership because it assured her even in the midst of fear, confusion, turmoil, and uncertainty that the appropriate actions and responses will somehow be revealed (Crawford, 2001; Williams, 1998).

On June 11, 1963, Hamer and several other civil rights workers were heading on a trip to Septima Clark's citizenship school in Charleston, South Carolina where they learned how to handle the voting registration process. Among this group were John Brown, Bernard Washington, Euvester Simpson, June Johnson, Rosemary Freeman, James West, Annelle Ponder, and Fannie Lou Hamer. They arrived in Winona, Mississippi for a restroom break and some in the group decided that they would use this trip to test the Interstate Commerce Commission ban on segregated bus terminals (Sitkoff, 1981). The real trouble started in Columbus, Mississippi where the group had abandoned their plans to integrate for fear of safety, but word spread across county lines in Mississippi and trouble was waiting for them in Winona. Earl Wayne Patridge was sheriff and had a rule: "any nigger dumb enough to challenge Jim Crow in Montgomery County got a whipping-no exceptions" (Lee, 2000, p. 48). Hamer stayed on the bus while some of the others attempted to get service in the café. The group was driven out of the diner by force. Annelle Ponder, a school teacher from Atlanta, began to write the license plates of the police cars. Looking out the bus window, Hamer rushed to help. She was kicked in the shins by a sheriff's deputy and taken into police custody.

The sheriff made a call to Ruleville to verify Hamer was from that town. Upon returning, she was told with a devilish grin "you're from Ruleville all right, you bitch, now we're gonna make you wish you was dead" (Lee, 2000, p. 51). The sheriff and his patrolman were too tired to dish out any more beatings, so they summoned two Black male inmates to perform the beatings on Hamer. She even tried to appeal to one of the men "you mean you would do this to your own race? (Lee, 2000, p. 51). Using Black men to do the dirty work was an old Mississippi tactic. The first inmate was handed a cosh, a lead pipe wrapped in leather with a flexible handle. She rolled on her belly to protect her weak side that was affected by an accident as a child. As the blows came, her legs were moving and shaking. The second inmate sat on her legs to keep her still. Her dress would rise and she would try to pull it down. But the overseeing deputy pulled her dress all the way up.

When one man would get tired, they would trade places. The beating went on until Hamer's flesh was oozing with huge gashes and cuts covered her body. Her hands were swollen turning Black and blue. She suffered permanent nerve damage in her left eye that caused blindness and her kidneys were permanently damaged.

Throughout this ordeal, she recalled the wife of the jailer being nice to her. Hamer asked the jailer to read two Bible verses,

- Though his hatred covers itself with guile, his wickedness will be revealed before the assembly. (Proverbs 26:26)
- Hath made of one blood all nations of men for to dwell on all the face of the earth, and hath determined the times before appointed, and the bounds of their habitations. (Acts 17:26)

This undoubtedly was a hellish three nights in jail for Hamer and the others who were savagely beaten. Nevertheless, Hamer was able to place this incident within a larger context of struggle, an unfolding civil rights battle in which she could fight on her own terms (Lee, 2000). Hamer had a prophetic transforming vision, grounded in resistance, a sense of moralism, and quest for democratic and equitable practice (Dantley, 2003). Critical servant leaders are receptive to the burdens of communities in distress. They actively pursue ways to transform and affect future outcomes by resisting the status quo and introducing opposition to unfair policies. As a critical servant leader, Hamer despised the current power structure. She, along with Victoria Gray and Annie Devine, articulated a plan for the radical reconstruction of the election process in Mississippi.

Political Enfranchisement: Personal Memory and Heartfelt Pain

In 1964, Hamer helped organize the Mississippi Freedom Democratic Party (MFDP) which was an alternative to the White controlled Democratic Party. The MFDP would run mock elections to show the power of the Black vote. The MFDP challenged the all

White Mississippi delegation at the 1964 Democratic National Convention in Atlantic City, New Jersey (Lee, 2000, 2001; Mills, 1993). During this upstaging, Hamer gave a heartfelt account of the violence she and other civil rights workers endured while attempting to register. She was very descriptive in the detail. News networks started a live broadcast, but President Lyndon B. Johnson scheduled a live address at the time, forcing networks to break away from her speech. Hamer closed her testimony, but it was later aired in full on the evening news. She challenged the establishment, including President Johnson, on the fact that the all-White delegation was illegal because not all of the citizens of Mississippi voted. Not to mention that most had connections to the Ku Klux Klan and supported the intimidating policies in Mississippi. She stated, "if the Freedom Democratic Party is not seated now, I question America (Crawford, 2001). She concluded her address with this rhetorical question:

> Is this America, the land of the free and the home of the brave where we have to sleep with our phones off the hooks because our lives be threatened daily because we want to live as decent human beings in America? If this is a great society, I'd hate to see a bad one. (Lee, 2000, p. 101)

Hamer became the conscience of the civil rights movement. She shamed White liberals in the Democratic Party who would not make room for the participation of Black Americans. Needless to say, there was a compromise that the MFDP would get two delegate seats and the all-White Mississippi delegation would remain intact. Hamer was incensed and said, "we didn't come all this way for no two seats" (Crawford, 2001, p. 133). This compromise drew a wedge between Hamer and the middle class Black leaders that supported the compromise.

Even though the MFDP failed to unseat the all-White delegation, their efforts had a lasting impact on the democratic process. She continued politically organizing. She was a delegate to the 1968 Democratic National Convention, where she rebuked authorities for failing to provide justice for Dr. Martin Luther King's assassination. She saved the worst of her wrath for elite

Blacks who supported what she called the "National Association for the Advancement of Certain People" (Lee, 2000). Hamer was bitterly disappointed with the Black middle class who she thought had forgotten about their people, yet she shared the same contempt for the poor rural Blacks who were often times too terrified to stand up for themselves (Lee, 2000).

Over the years her vision expanded to include economic development and health and nutrition education. The latter became very dear to her heart because her daughter Dorothy Jean died in 1967 from complications of malnutrition. It was not enough for Hamer to fight for inclusion in American society, but she sought to transform and improve American society. She measured this in terms of equal voting rights, adequate housing, minimum income standards, health care, and a decent diet (Lee, 2000). Unfortunately, Hamer did not see this transformation completed. She felt abandoned by the members of SNCC as she voted against a proposal to exclude Whites in the organization. Hamer refused to fight hatred with hatred in the civil rights war. She advocated equal rights for Blacks, but also invited poor Whites to join the struggle to secure a better future for themselves and their children (Williams, 1998). She relied on her faith and lived up to her moral principles. She felt dejected and felt they turned cold, distant, and unloving. She had taken it personally when the community that nurtured her early career had crumbled. Separatists in SNCC deemed Hamer no longer relevant to the movement.

In spite of the failures, disappointments, and her own personal problems, she turned her attention to fighting poverty. With donations, she established the Freedom Farm Cooperative that produced pounds of fresh vegetables and meats for Black farmers who were displaced by mechanization in Sunflower County (Lee, 2000; Mills, 1993). In 1969, 32% of Blacks in Sunflower County were on welfare, 70% percent lived in deteriorating homes, and 60% lacked indoor plumbing (Lee, 2000). Between 1969 and 1973, Freedom Farm successfully channeled federal money into building new homes and helped farm families secure social security income. Hamer's work with Freedom Farm literally saved people from starving to death. But fighting poverty was an uphill battle.

Freedom Farm was plagued with financial problems, as there was no one who was educated on how to manage and budget federal dollars. Freedom Farm went bankrupt in 1976. As her civil rights coalition and Freedom Farm deteriorated, she became increasingly disappointed.

As the end of her days neared, she wondered had she really made a difference in the democratic movement at all. Her husband Pap voiced his resentment and anger about the way his wife was treated in her last years. He said:

> I would come to this house and it would be so many people in here I couldn't hardly get in the door. They came to get clothes, food, money—everything. But when she fell sick and was in the hospital at Mound Bayou, the only way I could get people to stay with her was when I paid them. I tried to warn my wife, I told her "You can't do everything." But still they called on her...As soon as she got in [from a trip], they would call her again. They wore her down. She raised lots of money and she would come back and give it to people. And when she died, she didn't have a dime. (Sklar, 1989)

Even in her sickness and last days, Hamer was concerned with the local issues of economic development and political participation. She attended meetings when she was well and passed the leadership to the younger people. She said, "There's such a thing as loyalty and love, loyalty to my people and love for my people. And I love Ruleville" (Mills, 1993, p. 305). Her loyalty, love, and zeal are undeniable characteristics that aided her in the fight for civil rights. In 1977, at the age of 59, Mrs. Fannie Lou Hamer died from complications of breast cancer, hypertension, and a broken heart.

In the context of critical servant leadership, it is imperative to understand Hamer's personal life as it illuminates her passion and level of commitment to her political life as well. For Hamer the personal was political. Her life was a total commitment of critical service. Her vision was truly prophetic and is full with a myriad of successes and disappointments. Fannie Lou Hamer's life speaks to the physical pain, emotional pain, and spiritual foundation that formed her into the critical servant she was. She was forced to endure some extreme hardships because she was a Black woman who decided she wanted to live as a free and equal citizen in racist America.

Herstory–Septima Poinsette Clark: Liberating Minds through Literacy

Septima Poinsette Clark was born in 1898, thirty-five years after slavery was abolished in southern states (Brown, 1990; Clark, 1962). She was the second daughter of Peter Porcher Poinsette, a former slave and Victoria Warren Anderson, a Haitian American raised in Haiti. During her coming of age in Charleston, South Carolina, Septima Pointsette Clark would encounter the paradoxes of segregation and racism inside and outside of the home. These encounters shaped the critical servant leader she would become years later.

Life for Blacks in Charleston had been shaped by the gains and losses of political power after the Civil War and during reconstruction era (Charron, 2009). Freedom for Blacks at this time had come approximately thirty years earlier. The majority of the Black population lived in Low Country and was the epicenter of Black militancy and political activism (Charron, 2009). In 1867, Black voters elected Black city councilmen, congressmen, state legislators, senators, and delegates to the Republican convention. Blacks wielded political power within the Republican Party and attempted to forge an interracial democracy protected by the law. Among political power moves, Blacks established churches, schools, newspapers, mutual aid societies; all to defend their freedom, promote their autonomy, and train future leaders (Charron, 2009). Clark was surrounded by the reminders of such a rich history of Black success. Nevertheless, around the late 1870's, segregation which was practiced in the north prior to the Civil War was introduced in the south. Clark spent her childhood navigating the hostility of her environment driven by fear and hatefulness.

Nearly every success won by Black voters during reconstruction was repealed and again Blacks were relegated to second-class citizenship. Septima Clark's parents handled the recently enacted social system differently. Clark's father, a former slave, fought alongside his former master in the confederacy. Her father was a devout Christian, devoid of any animosity, and was willing to work hard to educate his children (Rouse, 2001). Education was very important to the Poinsette family. At one time, Peter Poinsette was an entrusted slave whose job was to accompany the Poinsette children to school, sit outside of the schoolhouse until they were complete with lessons, and accompany them back home. Mr. Poinsette's recognition of the importance of education developed as he never learned to read and write until he applied for a civil service job as a janitor and needed to sign his name. On the other hand, Victoria Poinsette was raised as a free person in Haiti, an independent Black controlled country. She was among the Haitian elite as her father was a prominent businessman. This upbringing gave her a strong sense of confidence and determination. It also contributed to her willingness to challenge aggressively all forms of racial oppression (Brown, 1990; Rouse, 2001).

Education: A Key to Political Liberation

It was well understood in the Clark household that education was central to autonomy, political liberation, and a sure way to fight racism and injustice. She attended public school until eighth grade. There were no public high schools for Blacks in Charleston at the time, so she and her family had to find a way to afford Avery Normal Institute, a private school for Blacks at $1.50 tuition per month. She finished Avery in 1916 at 18 years old with a licensure of instruction (which was equivalent to an associate's degree). She would teach on John's Island for the next three years. Clark was confronted with the most abject living conditions she had ever seen, and witnessed firsthand the impact that poverty, racism, and intra-group gender discrimination could have on the lives of Black people (Rouse, 2001). Septima was one of two teachers at a school with 132 students ranging from first to eighth grade (Hall & Walker, 2010). She quickly learned that the education cycle was determined by the contract between sharecroppers and landowners. The longer she stayed on John's Island, the more the young people expressed a desire to attend school and flee the life of poverty they had become accustomed to. She bonded with the local community as she was not only a teacher, but also became the inspiration that they needed to improve their lives. She taught children in the daytime and taught adults to read and write their names as well.

While teaching on John's Island, Septima Clark joined the movements to have Charleston hire Black teachers in public schools. In 1916, Charleston public schools would not hire Black teachers. It was during this time she joined the NAACP. She reflected on her experience:

> In all the public schools in Charleston, you know, we had White teachers teaching Black children. In 1919, we went door to door to ask people if they wanted Black teachers to teach their children. That was my first real political thing. Because the lawmakers said that only mulattoes wanted these jobs and they didn't think that the domestic workers and the chauffeurs and the garbage people and the longshoremen wanted Black teachers. So we had to do a door-to-door thing to get Black teachers to teach their children. And in 1920 we got them. Oh, that thing had been coming a long time, but we hadn't' gotten to the place where we felt as if we could get the signatures (20,000) before. I took my students along with me, and we got these signatures. Some would be across the street, and then I'd do it on the other side, and that's how we did it. (Clark, 1962; Hall & Walker, 2010)

Septima Clark was determined to do what she thought was right for Black children. In her expert opinion, drawing from the lived racialized experience in the south, she understood the cultural and pedagogical significance of having Black teachers teach Black students. But, we assume, she also believed that this would instill solidarity within the Black community as well. Clark's leadership at such an early part of her career speaks to the lessons she learned about the importance of education at home. From our research, we gather that Clark was a visionary and could foresee the reciprocal impact of her work.

Clark viewed herself as the embodiment of her parents' experiences and balanced perspectives. She could be compassionate and generous like her father, but she could also be tough, determined, and fearless like her mother. She learned three very important things that she accredits to her father; a strong belief in God, an education, and a willingness to serve those less fortunate (Clark, 1962; Rouse, 2001). These characteristics and attributes served her well in working with working rural class Black Americans, which was vital to the success her teaching career on Johns Island, the NAACP, the Highlander Folk School, Southern Christian Leadership Conference, and the Voter Education Project (Gyant & Atwater, 1996; Rouse, 2001).

"My first radical job": Challenging the Status Quo

In 1929, Septima Clark and the NAACP crusaded for the equalization of teacher's salaries in Charleston (Brown, 1990; Clark, 1962; Hall & Walker, 2010; Rouse, 2001). Black teachers were paid substantially less regardless of their qualifications or responsibilities. Many Black teachers were afraid to become involved with the NAACP lawsuit. But Septima Clark worked with NAACP lawyer Thurgood Marshall on the court case (Rouse, 2001). She later recalled in her biography:

> My participation in this fight was what might be described by some as my first radical job. I would call it my first effort in a social action challenging the status quo. I felt that in reality I was working for the accomplishment of something that ultimately would be good for everyone. (Clark, 1962, p. 82)

Clark's statement speaks volumes to her commitment to creating a better future for others. The court decision required teacher salaries to be equalized. However, the school authorities decided to require that teachers take a national exam, which was another hurdle for Black teachers. But Septima Clark passed and saw her salary triple. After winning this battle, she forged on to continue her education. She took classes in New York and Atlanta where she studied with W.E.B. DuBois who inspired her and reinforced the importance of dedicating her life to campaigns for social justice (Rouse, 2001). She went on to receive her bachelor's degree from Benedict College in 1942 and her master's from Hampton Institute in 1946 (Hall & Walker, 2010). She taught school for 18 years in Columbia, SC. Once again, during the day, she taught children, and at night, she taught adults. She moved back to Charleston to care for her ailing mother. During this time, her local leadership became apparent. She was active in the segregated ranks of the YWCA. Although she would attend interracial YWCA committee meetings, the organizations remained segregated by holding separate work meetings pertaining to the needs of their respective communities. Clark said in her autobiography that working with the YWCA taught her patience and the importance of keeping control of her temper (Clark, 1962).

Clark continued her work in local organizations. She was involved with the Charleston Federation of Women's Clubs, Metropolitan Council of Negro Women, and Alpha Kappa Alpha Sorority, Inc. The activities of these groups ranged from education to improving health care for children. Clark had always maintained her membership in the NAACP. In 1954, the landmark case *Brown v. Board of Education* was decided. The south was in an uproar and sought ways to retaliate. In 1956, the state legislature of South Carolina passed a law that no public employee could be a member of the NAACP or any other civil rights group (Clark, 1962; Hall & Walker, 2010; Robnett, 1996; Rouse, 2001). She listed her membership and was fired from her teaching job. She tried to get other Black teachers to go meet with the superintendent, but only eleven accompanied her.

"Through the fire and the flood": Citizenship and Voter Education

Though she had been fired from her previous teaching job, she was offered numerous jobs from all over the country, but she decided to be the Director of Workshops for the Highlander Folk School in Tennessee and work with social activist Myles Horton. Septima had previously attended and directed workshops at Highlander and begun to exert her influence before she became a staff member

(Robnett, 1996; Rouse, 2001). Highlander played a critical role in helping educate adults for citizenship because voting rights were still restricted in the south via literacy tests. Of those that attended Highlander workshops were Fannie Lou Hamer, Rosa Parks, Esau Jenkins, and many others who were vigilant in the fight for civil rights. Among literacy training, Highlander also taught courses on federal and state laws, constitutional rights, civil disobedience, and social change. Speakers for workshop series included Dr. King, Eleanor Roosevelt, college professors, and international visitors as well. Highlander was probably the only place in the south where Blacks and whites could organize and integrate.

Over the years, Clark's method of teaching was relevant to the uneducated population she served. She related subjects like math and English to the everyday problems they faced. She would teach adults to read by first recognizing street signs and by browsing the newspapers. She used this same method early in her career on John's Island as well as with her work with Southern Christian Leadership Conference (SCLC) (Gyant & Atwater, 1996). Clark developed citizenship schools early in her career at Highlander. She helped Esau Jenkins establish a citizenship school on John's Island with the help of her cousin Bernice Johnson, who taught night classes two nights a week (Clark, 1962). Within three years of the citizenship school opening on Johns Island, 600 Blacks had attended and registered to vote in Charleston County. The following year, with the help of Bernice Johnson and SCLC, Septima Clark developed a program to train teachers who would work all over the south teaching literacy to millions. By 1970, two million Black Americans had registered to vote (Clark, 1962; Gyant & Atwater, 1996; Rouse, 2001). Septima Clark was instrumental in two million Americans exercising their civil rights.

The state of Tennessee had been seeking ways to shut down Highlander, often referred to as communist headquarters. Septima Clark noted: "...anyone who was against segregation was considered a communist" (Brown, 1990, p. 55). Nevertheless, on trumped up charges of illegally selling liquor, Highlander's non-profit status was revoked, and after many court appeals, was closed and property seized by the state of Tennessee. Myles Horton and Septima Clark, among many other activists, knew the closure of Highlander was inevitable. Clark stated: "the Highlander at Monteagle as we knew it and love it, I have no doubt is finished...But I know that no person and no sovereign commonwealth will ever be able to take our Highlander from me" (Clark, 1962, p. 232).

So, much of the work was transferred to SCLC with Dr. King. Septima Clark, Andrew Young, and Dorothy Cotton traveled the south providing assistance with planning marches and establishing citizenship schools. Clark believed that it was necessary to peacefully break an unjust law. She supported the sit-ins by college students seeking an end to segregation (Clark, 1962). They would go into communities and recruit teachers for the citizenship schools. Septima Clark's goal was to help others find their voice and use it. Her life's purpose was to help others improve their lives and move toward self and community empowerment. In her autobiography, she remembered a woman whose money had been stolen out of her bank account. The woman didn't know how to write a check and depended on white people to do it for her. Clark's response was to have a banker come and speak to the group about how to write a check. Clark never let her education, status, or rank interfere with teaching people how to live with dignity despite their circumstances.

In 1962, the SCLC and four other civil rights groups combined talent and resources to form the Voter Education Project (Clark, 1962, 1980; Robnett, 1996, 1997; Rouse, 2001). Over the next four years, they prepared approximately 10,000 teachers for citizenship schools which were responsible for nearly 700,000 Black Americans registered to vote in the south. Each state had different laws, making voting difficult, so the courses were designed to educate future voters by state. Even though the Voting Rights Act was passed in 1965, the south was still in an uproar. But what disgruntled Clark the most was the fear and apathy of Black ministers and middle class Blacks who refused to participate in suffrage and community organizing. She stated:

I don't know whether they were afraid to try to teach others, or if they
had some highfalutin idea that poor people were so far beneath them
that they wouldn't fool with them. Many middle class Blacks were
extremely hostile and prejudiced one to the other. That's the way they
were.....we got them to see what conditions they were living under, but
we couldn't get them to do any work in their community to help others to
change. Couldn't get them to do that. That's the one big reason why, we
started the citizenship schools...It would be better to use people from the
community in which they lived who could just read well aloud and write
legibly, rather than trying to use the others. (Wiggington, 1992, p. 241 as
cited in Rouse, 2001)

Clark could not understand that frame of thinking and kept
doing the work. When asked was she fearful of retaliation, she
said: "No, I'm not afraid! I'm trying to do what I think is right and
I'm not afraid" (Clark, 1962, p. 115). Throughout the controversy of
her work, she remained calm, courageous, truthful, always seeing
something noble in everyone, and keeping her faith in God (Gyant
& Atwater, 1996). All along, Clark believed that "learning how to
read and write comes always this thing of becoming a responsible
citizen...One should know the laws and obey them for one's own
protection as well as for the protection of others" (Clark, 1962, p.
150). In her own words, "who can estimate the worth of pride
achieved, hope accomplished, faith affirmed, citizenship won?
(Clark, 1962, p. 154).

"Those men didn't have any faith in women":
Race and Gender

By 1970, Septima Clark retired from SCLC. She'd been through
the fire and the flood with education, citizenship, and civil rights.
She was humbled and proud of what she had accomplished with
others. She experienced racism as well as intra-group gender bias.
Through her work at SCLC, she endured hardships. She didn't
agree with the way she and women colleagues (Ella Baker,
Dorothy Cotton) were treated and how they had to take a backseat
in the decision making process (Crawford, et al., 1993; Robnett,
1996, 1997). She felt that men had little faith in women and saw
them more as sex symbols with little or no contributions to make
(Brown, 1990; Clark, 1962):

> I was on the executive staff of SCLC, but the men on it didn't listen to me too well. They liked to send me into many places because I could always make a path in to get people to listen to what I have to say. But those men didn't have any faith in women, none whatsoever. They just thought that women were sex symbols and had no contribution to make. That's why Rev. Abernathy would say continuously, "Why is Mrs. Clark on this staff? (Brown, 1990, p. 77)

Furthermore, Clark also discussed Dr. King's role in gender biases:

> Dr. King would say...Well she has expanded our program. She has taken it into eleven Deep South states. Rev. Abernathy'd come right back the next time and ask again. I don't think that he thought too much of me, because when I was in Europe with him, when he received the Nobel Peace prize in 1964, the American Friends Service Committee people wanted me to speak. In a sort of casual way he would say "Anything I can't answer, ask Mrs. Clark...I think that there is something among the Kings that makes them feel that they are the kings and so you don't have a right to speak. You can work behind the scenes all you want...But don't come forth and try to lead. That's not the kind of thing they wanted (Brown, 1990, pp. 77-78).

Part of what Septima Clark and other women experienced in the civil rights movement was the traditions of men, Black and White, controlling public social space (Gyant & Atwater, 1996). Women like Clark were all too aware of the role of women ascribed to them by their gender and for Black women, their gender and race. Clark reflected and said:

> I sent a letter to Dr. King asking him not to lead all the marches himself, but instead develop leaders who could lead their marches. Dr. King read that letter before the staff. It just tickled them; they just laughed....but in those days I didn't criticize Dr. King, other than asking him not to lead all the marches. I adored him. I supported him because I greatly respected his courage, his service to others, and his non-violence. The way I think about him now comes from my experience in the women's movement. But in those days, of course, in the Black church men were always in charge. It was just the way things were. Like other Black ministers, Dr. King didn't think too much about the way women could contribute. But working in the movement, he changed the lives of so

many people that getting to the place where he would have to see women are more than sex symbols. I see this as one of the weaknesses of the civil rights movement, the way the men looked at women. (Brown, 1990, pp. 78-79)

The feelings Clark addresses did not stop her or women such as Fannie Lou Hamer, Ella Baker, Dorothy Cotton, and others from doing the work of the movement. It only gave them fuel to keep pushing because they knew what needed to be done for the best interests of the community (Gyant & Atwater, 1996).

Clark's approach to critical servant leadership was tempered and strategic. She challenged the status quo using the tools of citizenship and tools of administrations that vowed to stop progress. It was through her ability to relate to others, to build community, and inspire while never forgetting the overarching prophetic vision to seize opportunities for first class citizenship. Even though we hail Septima Poinsette Clark as the queen mother of the civil rights movement, she preferred not to have a title.

I do not like to be described as a Negro leader fighting for the integration of the schools, the churches, the transportation facilities, the political parties, or whatnot. I don't consider myself a fighter, I'd prefer to be looked on as a worker, a woman who loves her fellow man, white and Negro alike and yellow, red, and brown, and is striving with her every energy, working–not fighting—in the true spirit of fellowship to lift him to a higher level of attainment and appreciation and enjoyment of life. (Clark, 1962, p. 131)

Clark was a critical servant leader as she dedicated her life to improving the status of Black Americans. Teaching Blacks to read, write, and vote was a dangerous concept (Gyant & Atwater, 1996). She knowingly committed herself to educating and liberating with literacy. Because of her commitment and dedication, she has left a legacy of activism, critical service, and spirited leadership. She understood and lived the meaning of the African proverb, "I am because we are. We are because I am" (Gyant & Atwater, 1996).

Leadership Praxis

In many ways, this chapter demonstrates the variety and complexity of practicing leadership as Black women in such a hostile time. Through the autobiographical accounts we see different approaches with these women. Fannie Lou Hamer challenged the status quo outside of the system by agitating the powers that be through charged vocalization of mistreatment, abuse, and disenfranchisement. However, Septima Clark challenged the system of injustice through more tempered means such as voter education and working within prominent organizations that afforded her the shield of security from retaliation. Neither approach is better than the other. However, the application of leadership comes from their lived experience which caused them to interpret and apply leadership differently. Their gendered experiences were apparent in their stories; however, their class status at the time defined the life they lived. Thankfully, their class status did not define how they led during times of adversity. Their leadership legacies were inclusive of all people; in particular of all Black people regardless of gender and/or class position

An ultimate test of leadership is in applying it to situations that seemed irresolvable (Trompenaars & Voerman, 2010). Clark and Hamer were tested because they faced a daunting task. Yet they were not deterred. One may ask, what is the secret of a servant leader or critical servant leader? (Trompenaars & Voerman, 2010). From researching the lives of these women, we would say that the secret of their leadership praxis is the absence of "the best way" or "the right way" (p. 27) to achieve the desired goal(s). Their willingness to serve, which was guided by their lived experiences, resonated through all of their actions and interactions with people. Through their leadership praxis, they were able to transform the tension of civil rights work into a productive and dynamic endeavor. By serving with intent, spiritual steadfastness, and integrity, they became stronger as women leaders, thus giving room for others to grow as leaders and first rate citizens during this tumultuous period.

Points to Consider

1. The servant leader concept is a paradox to some and represents a dilemma. Upon reviewing the lives of. Fannie Lou Hamer and Septima Clark, can you identify the dilemma or paradox of their leadership praxis?

2. Can you assess the magnitude of the risks Clark and Hamer undertook as servant leaders/critical servant leaders? Would you be willing to take the same risks for others?

3. Septima Clark discussed her (mis)treatment by men in the civil rights movement because of her gender. This concept of gender discrimination in leadership is certainly not an anomaly within the Black community. In your opinion, what has changed in terms of gender dynamics across the board?

4. Fannie Lou Hamer and Septima Clark were both critical servant leaders. In your assessment of their leadership lives, discuss how the intersections of race and gender had an impact on their application of leadership.

Suggested Readings

Asch, C. M. (2008). *The senator and the sharecropper. The freedom struggles of James O. Eastland and Fannie Lou Hamer.* New York: New Press.

Barnett, B. M. (1993). Invisible southern Black women leaders in the civil rights movement: The triple constraints of gender, race, and class. *Gender & Society, 7*(2), 162-182.

Brown, C. S. (Ed.). (1990). *Ready from within, a first person narrative: Septima Clark and the civil rights movement.* Trenton, NJ: Africa World Press, Inc.

Charron, K. M. (2009). *Freedom's teacher: The life of Septima Clark.* Chapel Hill, NC: The University of North Carolina Press

Childs, J. B. (1989). *Leadership, conflict, and cooperation in Afro-American social thought.* Philadelphia: Temple University Press.

Clark, S. P. (1962). *Echo in my soul.* New York: E. P. Dutton & Co., Inc.

Clark, S. P. (1980). Citizenship and gospel. *Journal of Black Studies, 10*(4), 461-466.

Clark, S. P. (1986). *Ready from within: Septima Clark and the civil rights movement.* Navarro, CA: Wild Tree Press.

Crawford, V. L. (2001). African American women in the Mississippi Freedom Democratic Party. In B. Collier-Thomas & V. P. Franklin (Eds.), *Sisters in the struggle: African American women in the civil rights-Black power movement* (pp. 121-138). New York: New York University Press.

Crawford, V. L., Rouse, J. A., & Woods, B. (Eds.). (1993). *Women in the civil rights movement: Trailblazers and torchbearers, 1941-1965.* Bloomington, IN: Indiana University Press.

Gyant, L., & Atwater, D. F. (1996). Septima Clark's rhetorical and ethnic legacy: Her message of citizenship in the civil rights movement. *Journal of Black Studies, 26*(5), 577-592.

Hall, J., & Walker, E. P. (2010). I train the people to do their own talking: Septima Clark and women in the civil rights movement. *Southern Cultures, 1*(1), 31-52.

Hamer, F. L. (1969). Speech to the systematic training and redevelopment program. Jackson, MS: Audiovisual Collection of the Mississippi Department of Archives and History.

Hine, D. C. (Ed.). (1993). *Black women in America* (Vol. 1-2). Brooklyn, NY: Carlson Publishers.

Lee, C. K. (2000). *For freedom's sake: The life of Fannie Lou Hamer.* Chicago: University of Illinois Press.

Lee, C. K. (2001). Anger, memory, and personal power: Fannie Lou Hamer and civil rights leadership. In B. Collier-Thomas & V. P. Franklin (Eds.), *Sisters in the struggle: African American women in the civil rights–Black power movement* (pp. 139-170). New York: New York University Press.

McClellan, P. (2010). Toward critical servant leadership in graduate schools of education: From theoretical construct to social justice praxis. In S. D. Horsford (Ed.), *New perspectives in educational leadership: Exploring social, political, and community contexts and meanings.* New York: Peter Lang Publishing.

Mills, K. (1993). *This little light of mine: The life of Fannie Lou Hamer.* New York: Penguin Books.

Paris, P. J. (1995). *The spirituality of African peoples: The search for a common moral discourse.* Minneapolis: Fortress Press.

Payne, C. M. (1995). *I've got the light of freedom: The organizing and the Mississippi freedom struggle.* Berkeley, CA: University of California Press.

Raines, H. (1977). *My soul is rested.* New York: Penguin Books.

Roberts, D. (1997). *Killing the Black body: Race, reproduction, and the meaning of liberty.* New York: Vintage Books.

Rosenberg, P. S. (1992). *Race, class and gender in the United States: An integrated study* (2 ed.). New York: St. Martins Press.

Walker, V. S., & Snarey, J. R. (Eds.). (2004). *Race-ing moral formation: African American perspectives on care and justice.* New York: Teachers College Press.

Walters, R. W., & Smith, R. C. (1999). *African American leadership.* Albany, NY: State University of New York Press.

Wiegman, R. (1995). *American anatomies: Theorizing race and gender.* Durham, NC: Duke University Press.

Wiggington, E. (Ed.). (1992). *Refuse to stand silently by: An oral history of grass roots social activism in America, 1921-1964.* New York: Doubleday.

Williams, L. E. (1998). *Servants of the people: The 1960's legacy of African American leadership.* New York: St. Martin's Press.

Video Resources: Teaching/learning tools to be used as supplementary material to support and expand the given topic.

- *Braveheart* (1995) – featuring Mel Gibson, James Robinson, and Shawn Lawler
- Building Servant Leaders to Transform Organizations: http://www.forthesakeofothers.com/videos/
- *Fannie Lou Hamer: Everyday Battle* (DVD, 2004)

- *Fannie Lou Hamer*–Testimony at the 1964 Democratic National Convention: http://www.zimbio.com/watch/xcXxeM0SJF/Fannie+Lou+H amer+Testimony+1964+Democratic/A+Celebration+of+Wo men%27s+History
- *Fannie Lou Hamer: Voting Rights Activists & Civil Rights Leader* (DVD, 2010): http://www.tmwmedia.com/Black_american_experience.htm l or http://www.amazon.com
- *Good Will Hunting* (1997) – featuring Matt Damon and Ben Affleck
- Ken Melrose on Servant Leadership: http://www.baylor.edu/business/index.php?id=45605
- Martin Luther King on Servant Leadership: http://www.leadership-with-you.com/servant-leadership-video.html
- *Patch Adams* (1998) – featuring Robin Williams, Daniel London, and Monica Potter
- Tom Peters on Servant Leadership: http://www.tompeters.com/dispatches/011561.php

References

Alston, J. (2000). Missing in action: Where are the Black female school superintendents? *Urban Education, 35*(5), 525-531.

Alston, J. (2005). Tempered radicals and servant leaders: Black females preservering in the superintedency. *Education Adminstration Quarterly, 41*(4), 675-700.

Barnett, B. M. (1993). Invisible southern Black women leaders in the civil rights movement: The triple constraints of gender, race, and class. *Gender & Society, 7*(2), 162-182.

Brooks, M. P. & Houck, D. W. (Eds.). (2011). *The speeches of Fannie Lou Hamer*. Jackson, MS: University Press of Mississippi.

Brown, C. S. (Ed.). (1990). *Ready from within, a first person narrative: Septima Clark and the civil rights Mmvement.* Trenton, NJ: Africa World Press, Inc.

Charron, K. M. (2009). *Freedom's Teacher: The life of Septima Clark.* Chapel Hill, NC: The University of North Carolina Press.

Childs, J. B. (1989). *Leadership, conflict, and cooperation in Afro-American social thought.* Philadelphia: Temple University Press.

Clark, S. P. (1962). *Echo in my soul.* New York: E. P. Dutton & Co., Inc.

Clark, S. P. (1980). Citizenship and gospel. *Journal of Black Studies, 10*(4), 461-466.

Clark, S. P. (1986). *Ready from within: Septima Clark and the Civil Rights Movement.* Navarro, CA: Wild Tree Press.

Collier-Thomas, B., & Franklin, V. P. (Eds.). (2001). *Sisters in the struggle: African American women in the civil rights-black power movement.* New York: New York University Press.

Collins, P. H. (1996). The social construction of Black feminist thought. In A. Garry & M. Pearsall (Eds.), *Women, knowledge and reality: Explorations in feminist philosophy* (pp. 222-248). New York and London: Routledge.

Collins, P. H. (1998). *Fighting words: Black women and the search for justice.* Minneapolis: University of Minnesota Press.

Collins, P. H. (2000). *Black feminist thought: Knowledge, consciousness, and the politics of empowerment* (Vol. 10). New York: Routledge.

Collins, P. H. (2004). Learning from the outsider-within: The sociological significance of Black feminist thought. In S. Harding (Ed.), *The feminist standpoint theory reader: Intellectual and political controversies* (pp. 103-126). New York and London: Routledge.

Crawford, V. L. (2001). African American women in the Mississippi Freedom Democratic Party. In B. Collier-Thomas & V. P. Franklin (Eds.), *Sisters in the struggle: African American women in the civil rights-Black power movement* (pp. 121-138). New York: New York University Press.

Crawford, V. L., Rouse, J. A., & Woods, B. (Eds.). (1993). *Women in the civil rights movement: Trailblazers and torchbearers, 1941-1965.* Bloomington, IN: Indiana University Press.

Dantley, M. (2003). Critical spirituality: Enhancing transformative leadership through critical theory and African American prophetic spirituality. *International Journal of Leadership in Education, 6*(3), 3-17.

Davis, A. Y. (1981). *Women, race, and class.* New York: Random House.

Davis, M. (Ed.). (1982). *Contributions of Black women in America* (Vol. 1). Columbia, SC: Kenday Press.

DeYoung, C. P. (2004). *Mystic-activists: Faith-inspired leaders working for social justice and reconciliation.* Ed.D. dissertation, University of St. Thomas (Minnesota).

Drath, W. H., & Palus, C. J. (1994). *Making common sense: Leadership as meaning-making in a community of practice.* Greensboro, NC: Center for Creative Leadership.

Edgerton, J. (1970). *A mind to stay here: Profiles from the South.* New York: Macmillan.

Eicher-Catt, D. (2005). The myth of servant leadership: A feminist perspective. *Women and Language, 28*(1), 17-25.

Greene, G. C. (2001). *Working toward literacy for a new social order: Human agency and the curriculum work of Septima Poinsette Clark, 1898--1987.* Ed.D. dissertation, University of South Carolina.

Greenleaf, R. K. (1977). *Servant leadership: A journey into the nature of legitimate power and greatness.* Ramsey, New Jersey: Paulist Press.

Gyant, L., & Atwater, D. F. (1996). Septima Clark's rhetorical and ethnic legacy: Her message of citizenship in the civil rights movement. *Journal of Black Studies, 26*(5), 577-592.

Hall, J., & Walker, E. P. (2010). I train the people to do their own talking: Septima Clark and women in the civil rights movement. *Southern Cultures, 1*(1), 31-52.

Hamer, F. L. (1969). Speech to the systematic training and redevelopment program. Jackson, MS: Audiovisual Collection of the Mississippi Department of Archives and History.

Hine, D. C. (Ed.). (1993). *Black women in America* (Vol. 1-2). Brooklyn, NY: Carlson Publishers.

Hine, D. C., & Thompson, K. (1998). *A shining thread of hope: The history of Black women in America.* New York: Broadway Books.

Holvino, E. (2010). Intersections: The simultaneity of race, gender, and class in organization studies. *Gender, Work, and Organization, 17*(3).

hooks, b. (1981). *Ain't I a woman: Black women and feminism.* Boston: South End Press.

hooks, b. (1984). *Feminist theory from margin to center.* Boston: South End Press.

Hull, G. T., & Scott, P. B. (Eds.). (1982). *All the women are white, All the Blacks are men: But some of us are brave.* Old Westbury, New York: The Feminist Press.

Jackson-Weaver, K. *Lift every voice: Black women's invisible leadership and faith during the civil rights era, 1955-1965.* Ph.D. dissertation, Columbia University

Jenkins, C. J., & Eckert, C. M. (1986). Channeling Black insurgency: Elite patronage and professional social movements' organizations in the development of the Black movement. *American Sociological Review, 51*(1), 812-829.

Jordan, A. *Faith in action: The first Citizenship School on Johns Island, South Carolina.* M.A. dissertation, East Tennessee State University, United States, Tennessee. Retrieved December 20, 2010, from Dissertations & Theses: A&I. (Publication No. AAT 1458315).

Lawson, S. P., & Payne, C. M. (Eds.). (1998). *Debating the civil rights movement, 1945-1968.* Lanham, MD: Rowman & Littlefield.

Lee, C. K. (1993). *A passionate pursuit of justice: The life and leadership of Fannie Lou Hamer, 1917-1967.* Ph.D. dissertation, University of California, Los Angeles

Lee, C. K. (2000). *For freedom's sake: The life of Fannie Lou Hamer.* Chicago: University of Illinois Press.

Lee, C. K. (2001). Anger, memory, and personal power: Fannie Lou Hamer and civil rights leadership. In B. Collier-Thomas & V. P. Franklin (Eds.), *Sisters in the struggle: African American women in the civil right-Black power movement* (pp. 139-170). New York: New York University Press.

Lubiano, W. (1992). Black ladies, welfare queens and the state minstrels: Ideological war by narrative means. In T. Morrison (Ed.), *Race-ing, En-gendering power* (pp. 321-361). New York: Pantheon Books.

McClellan, P. (2006). *Wearing the mantle: Spirited Black male servant leaders reflect on their leadership journey.* Ed.D. dissertation, Bowling Green State University, Bowling Green.

McClellan, P. (2010). Toward critical servant leadership in graduate schools of education: From theoretical construct to social justice praxis. In S. D. Horsford (Ed.), *New perspectives in educational leadership: Exploring social, political, and community contexts and meanings.* New York: Peter Lang Publishing.

Mills, K. (1993). *This little light of mine: The life of Fannie Lou Hamer.* New York: Penguin Books.

Moore, K. "S*he who learns, teaches": Black women teachers of the 1964 Mississippi Freedom Schools.* Ph.D. dissertation, The University of North Carolina at Chapel Hill.

Murtadha-Watts, K. (1999). Spirited sisters: Spirituality and the activism of African American women in educational leadership. In L. T. Fenwick & P. Jenlink (Eds.), *School leadership: Expanding the horizons of the mind and spirit* (pp. 155-167). Lancaster: Technomic Publishing Company, Inc.

Nadesan, M. H. (1999). The discourses of corporate spiritualism and evangelical capitalism. *Management Communication Quarterly, 13*(1), 3-42.

Parker, P. S. (2005). *Race, gender, and leadership: Re-envisioning organizational leadership from the perspectives of African American women executives.* Mawhah, New Jersey: Lawrence Erlbaum Associates.

Parker, P. S., & Olgivie, D. T. (1996). Gender, culture, and leadership: Toward a culturally distinct model of African-American women executives' leadership strategies. *Leadership Quarterly, 7*(2), 189-214.

Parker Brooks, M. *From the front porch to the platform: Fannie Lou Hamer and the rhetoric of the Black freedom movement.* Ph.D. dissertation, The University of Wisconsin-Madison, United States -- Wisconsin. Retrieved December 20, 2010, from Dissertations & Theses: A&I. (Publication No. AAT 3367793).

Payne, C. M. (1995). *I've got the light of freedom: The organizing and the Mississippi freedom struggle.* Berkely, CA: University of California Press.

Peacock, J. *Geographies of mentorship: Black women and the civil rights movement, a case study of Septima Clark and Ella Barker.* M.A. dissertation, University of Louisville, United States. Retrieved December 20, 2010, from Dissertations & Theses: A&I.(Publication No. AAT 1459531).

Raines, H. (1977). *My soul is rested.* New York: Penguin Books.

Robnett, B. (1996). African American women in the civil rights movement, 1954-1965: Gender, leadership, and microbilization. *American Journal of Sociology, 101*(6), 1661-1693.

Robnett, B. (1997). *How long? How long? African American women in the struggle for civil rights.* New York: Oxford University Press.

Rouse, J. A. (2001). "We seek to know...in order to speak the truth": Nurturing the seeds of discontent - Septima P. Clark and participatory leadership. In B. Collier-Thomas & V. P. Franklin (Eds.), *Sisters in the struggle: African American women in the civil rights--black power movement.* New York: New York University Press.

Russell, R., & Stone, A. G. (2002). A review of servant leadership attributes: Developing a practical model. *Leadership & Organizational Development Journal, 23*(3), 145-157.

Sendjaya, S., & Sarros, J. C. (2002). Servant leadership: Its origin, development, and application in organizations. *Journal of Leadership and Organization Studies, 9*(2), 57-64.

Sitkoff, H. (1981). *The struggle for Black equality, 1954-1980.* New York: Hill and Wange.

Sklar, B. (1989, November 20). Interview with Pap Hamer, November 20, 1989.

Spears, L. C. (Ed.). (1995). *Reflections on servant leadership.* New York: John Wiley & Sons, Inc.

Spencer, J. M. (1987). Freedom songs of the civil rights movement. *Journal of Black Sacred Music, 14.*

Sterling, D. (1979). *Black foremothers: Three lives.* Old Westbury, NY: Feminist Press.

Trompenaars, F., & Voerman, E. (2010). *Servant leadership across cultures.* Oxford: Infinite Ideas.

Truth, S. (1851). Ain't I a woman? *Women's rights convention.* Akron, Ohio.

Walker, A. (1983). *In search of our mother's garden.* New York: Harcourt.

Wiggington, E. (Ed.). (1992). *Refuse to stand silently by: An oral history of grass roots social activism in America, 1921-1964.* New York: Doubleday.

Williams, L. E. (1998). *Servants of the people: The 1960's legacy of African American Leadership.* New York: St. Martin's Press.

Young, P. D. (1976). A surfeit of surgery. *Washington Post, May 30, 1976,* p. B1.

Transformational Leadership: A Legacy of Faith and Service

Transformational leadership is one of the current approaches that has been the focus of a majority of research studies since the early 1980's (Northouse, 2007) amidst the rise of attention paid to the civil rights, anti-war, and women's liberation movements in scholarly circles. According to modern theorists, transformational leadership is part of the "new" leadership paradigm (Bryman, 1992) which gives more attention to the charismatic and affective elements of leadership. However, in our research for this book, we have found that transformational leadership is not a new leadership phenomenon in theory or practice. Yet, what we have noticed is that the leadership phenomenon has been conceptualized, theorized, and applied in current contexts and understandings of leadership behaviors of White males. However, quite to the contrary, many authors explicitly refer to transformational leadership as a "feminine" leadership style (e.g. Carless, 1998; Helgesen, 1990; Loden, 1985; Yammarino, Dubinsky, Comer, & Jolson, 1997). Therefore, our goal is to highlight two historical and prominent Black women who represent authentic transformational leadership. In doing so, we demonstrate transformational leadership as practiced in a historical context, while also posing serious questions about the exclusion of Black women from the leadership research and scholarship.

According to modern theorists (Bass & Avolio, 1994; Bass & Riggio, 2006; Lowe & Gardner, 2001), transformational leadership fits the needs of today's work groups and employees, who want to be inspired and empowered to succeed in time of uncertainty

(Northouse, 2007). This statement holds true when looking at transformational leaders in a historical context as well. In the time of racial and political unrest prior to and during the civil rights movement, the masses of underprivileged Black citizens needed leaders to inspire and empower in times of uncertainty. Mary McLeod Bethune and Shirley Chisholm accepted the clarion call for leadership. However, their stories in lieu of traditional leadership theories and traditional white and male leadership examples have been excluded. Clearly, many scholars are studying transformational leadership and transformational leaders, and the genre occupies a central place in leadership research, as do and should the stories of Mary McLeod Bethune and Shirley Chisholm.

Transformational Leadership Defined

Transformational leadership implies a process that changes and transforms people (Burns, 1978; Northouse, 2007). Primarily, transformational leadership is concerned with the values, ethics, and long-term goals that include assessing followers' motives, satisfying their needs, and treating them as human beings (Bass & Riggio, 2006; Burns, 1978; Northouse, 2007) instead of pawns. Being a transformational leader involves an exceptional form of influence (Northouse, 2007) which should not be taken lightly. Burns (1978) stated the magnitude of leadership influence eloquently when he said:

> Leaders are a particular kind of power holder. Like power, leadership is relational, collective, and purposeful. Leadership shares with power the central function of achieving purpose. But the reach and domain of leadership are, in the short range at least, more limited than those of power. Leaders do not obliterate followers' motives though they may arouse certain motives and ignore others. They lead. To control things—tools, mineral resources, money, energy—is an act of power, not leadership, for things have no motives. Power wielders may treat people as things. Leaders may not. (p. 18)

The transformational leader's role is vital to upholding a stern code of ethics and morality as well as being a humble steward over the responsibility and power she is given. According to Burns

(1978), leadership is a process of morality to the degree that leaders engage with followers on the basis of shared motives and values, and goals–on the basis of the followers' "true" needs as well as those of the leaders: psychological, economic, safety, or spiritual (p. 36). Although the transformational leader supplies the initiatives to spark change and transformation, ultimately, only the followers themselves can define their true needs. In essence, the follower and leader are inextricably linked in the transformation process (Northouse, 2007) through their shared motives, values, and goals. Additionally, Lewis (1996) noted that transformational leaders:

1. build on the strengths of others, strengths that may have lain dormant;
2. raise levels of awareness about the issues of consequence and ways of reaching organizational goals for their colleagues, subordinates, followers, clients, or constituents;
3. enable people to transcend their own self-interest for the sake of others;
4. change reality by building on the human need for meaning; focus on values, morals and ethics; are proactive and encourage human potential;
5. transform people and organizations—change minds and hearts; enlarge vision, insight and understanding, clarify purposes, make behavior congruent with beliefs, principles, or values; and bring about changes that are permanent, self-perpetuating, and momentum building;
6. bind people together around a common identity—goals and values; and
7. build for tomorrow what will be needed by the organization at that time.

While the term "transformational leadership" was coined by Downton in 1973, Burns extended the concept by linking the roles of the leader and the follower. Burns (1978) defined transformational leadership as the process of engaging with others and creating a connection that raises the level of motivation and morality of the leader and the follower. He set forth a conceptualization of transformational leadership that included raising the level of morality in others. He stated, "the leader is more skillful in evaluating followers' motives, anticipating their responses to an initiative and estimating their power bases than the reverse" (p. 20). This perception of the leader's superiority is promoted as Burns assumes that leaders take the major part or play in maintaining and articulating the relationship with followers as well as assuming the responsibility for "ultimately carrying out the combined purpose of leaders and followers" (Burns 1978, p. 20 as cited in Dantley, 2003a). By making this assumption, philosophically, there is a shift in the delineation of the lived leadership experiences of Black historical leaders at the time who were leaders, but also were part of the masses.

The Four I's of Transformational Leadership

Burns's (1979) theory of transformational leadership is founded on the notion that conditions of injustice spark the need for social change and a contention that transformational leaders intrinsically motivate followers to function as a collective to achieve a common goal. Furthermore, it is critical that the shared goal is inherently an ethical aim for social change and justice, anchored in the moral commitment to bring about social reform. The means do not justify the ends; transforming leaders are "burdened" with an ethical imperative to act morally (p. 202). "Moral leadership emerges from, and always returns to, the fundamental wants and needs, aspirations, and values of the followers...the kind of leadership that can produce social change that will satisfy followers' authentic needs" (p. 4). Thus, it is within this context where Avolio, Waldmen, and Yammarino (1991) found that transformational leadership behaviors consisted of four dimensions: a) Idealized influence (Charisma), b) Inspirational motivation (Inspiration), c) Intellectual stimulation, and d) Individualized consideration.

Leaders who exhibit *idealized influence* have the ability to encourage followers to accept radical change. These leaders are also said to be charismatic and possess charismatic vision and behavior that inspires others to follow. Here, individuals usually have strong moral and ethical conduct and high standards. As Northouse (2007) noted, Nelson Mandela is such a leader because "his charismatic qualities and the people's response to them transformed an entire nation" (p. 183).

Secondly, leaders can act with *inspirational motivation* to inspire followers to reach new heights. They possess a capacity to motivate others to commit to the vision. Antonakis and House (2002) described inspirational leaders as persons "who inspire and motivate followers to reach ambitious goals that may have previously seemed unreachable, by raising followers' expectations and communicating confidence that followers can achieve ambitious goals, thus creating self-fulfilling prophecy" (pp. 9-10).

When *intellectual stimulation* occurs, it moves and motivates followers toward innovation and creativity that is based on self-reflection. Northouse (2007) found that intellectual leadership supports followers as they try new approaches and develop innovative ways of dealing with organizational issues.

Finally, *individual consideration* occurs through the leader's analysis of her or his followers. These leaders act as coaches to the specific needs of followers. This includes the ability to diagnose followers' needs, values, and abilities. For example, Antonakis and House (2002) stated, "Leaders who provide customized socio-economic support to followers, while developing and empowering them. This outcome is achieved by coaching and counseling followers, maintaining frequent contact with them, and helping them to self-actualize" (pp. 9-10).

Transformational Leadership and Black Women Leaders

While Burns conceptualized leadership as a moral endeavor, this concept was fairly new in leadership research. However, historically and generally speaking, this separation rarely existed in the Black leadership experience (Dantley, 2003a, 2003b, 2005;

Dantley & Tillman, 2010; McClellan, 2006), in particular to that of Black women leaders (Clark, 1962; Collier-Thomas & Franklin, 2001; Generett & Jeffries, 2003; Jordan, 1972). Therefore, what we see in historical depictions of Black women leaders is zealousness, determination, and overarching radical implementation in their leadership practice; all of which are grounded in morality. New and inherently different voices must be added to the leadership discourse for substantive transformation to take place (Dantley, 2003a). Whether these women are identified as servant leaders, social justice leaders, or even transformational leaders, a common thread that flows through their leadership is their spiritual fervor.

The spiritual foundation and steadfastness of the women studied in this text used their foundation in their faith as an internal barometer that prodded their sense of justice and fairness. According to Stewart (1999), the Africana/Black spiritual experience has created a quest for human freedom not precipitated and shaped by political or social realities, but by people's capacity to create their own spirituality of culture in response to oppression, thus combating and transcending its myriad devastations (p.3). Similarly, Dantley (2003a) stated that a missing link in the transformational leadership literature is a spirit-filled resistance that proposes a project or praxis for institutional change. The leadership lives of Mary McLeod Bethune and Shirley Chisholm fill this gap. They were transformational leaders who were guided by their faith in God and the belief that as God's children, Black Americans deserve the full rights of American citizenship.

Herstory–Mary McLeod Bethune: Five Dollars, Faith, and a Fervent Vision

Mary Jane McLeod Bethune is one of America's most honored and distinguished women of the 19th and 20th centuries. Her accomplishments are numerous and the impact of her visionary transformative leadership immeasurable. Mary McLeod Bethune was born July 10, 1875 to former slaves Samuel and Patsy McIntosh McLeod. She was child number 15 of 17. Her legacy and leadership is one of determination, vision, will, and faith. From the beginning in Mayesville, South Carolina, Janie as she was affectionately called by family saw and lived the harsh realities at the intersections of being poor, uneducated, and Black. Although this was her reality for some time, Bethune envisioned a life for herself and others that would defy the unwritten rules and customs of the South.

Bethune always had a desire to read and write. Most of her siblings as well as her parents were born into slavery. They lacked the education and skills to be fully integrated into society post-Civil War era (Hanson, 2003). Despite the efforts of Freedmen's Bureau and missionary societies, illiteracy remained rampant among Black South Carolinians. In 1880, 78.5% of Blacks were illiterate compared to 21.99% of Whites (Hanson, 2003). Mary McLeod Bethune lived in Sumter County, which was a rural county where literacy statistics tended to be worse due to the political landscape at the time and the dependence on sharecropping and/or indenture servitude in the fields as a primary source of economic stability.

In many parts of the South, Sumter County included, a small White minority controlled the social, political, and economic livelihood of the poor, uneducated Black majority (Hanson, 2003). The McLeods were not exempt from the past slavery sharecropping system. However, it must be noted that the McLeods were atypical in that they eventually saved $30 and purchased the land on which they farmed. Racial experiences coupled with familial religious convictions fueled Mary McLeod Bethune's desire to learn. One pivotal example Bethune recalled in an interview with Charles Johnson:

> ...I remember my mother went over to do some special work for the family of Wilsons, and I was with her. I went out into what they called their play house in the yard where they did their studying. They had pencils, slates, magazines, and books. I picked up one of the books...and one of the girls said to me, "you can't read that—put that down." I will show you some pictures over here and when she said to me "you can't read that—put that down" it just did something to my pride and to my heart that made me feel that some day I would read as she was reading. (Johnson interview, 1940 as cited in McCluskey & Smith, 2001, p. 41)

Bethune said she relived that experience daily and used it as ammunition in her journey for education and self-empowerment. That incident drove home the connection between illiteracy and racial inequality (McCluskey & Smith, 2001).

She attended a one-room school house in Mayesville which was run by Presbyterian missionaries. Her first teacher was Emma Jane Wilson, a fair-skinned Black woman who became a significant mentor. Bethune was so eager to learn that she walked five miles to and from school to attend. After her lessons, she would then teach her siblings what she had learned in school. From early on, her education career blossomed, as she became the young woman in the community that Blacks and poor Whites would go to make sure their accounts were settled with dealers and brokers in an effort to make sure the poor and illiterate were not being cheated. Eventually, she started keeping family accounts and they were able to pay off their mortgage. She completed school by the age of 12. From there she attended Scotia Seminary (now Barbara Scotia College) through a scholarship donation by a Quaker seamstress. Bethune long believed that her leadership and life legacy would be by paying it forward.

While attending Scotia College, Bethune's leadership skills began to flourish. She organized social events for the causes of the day. In addition, she was also an intercessor between students and administrators on problems that plagued the girls during residency. In her interview with Charles Johnson, Bethune spoke of her school years at Scotia and said:

> ...homesick girls would always find me. Girls with their problems, difficulties, and disappointments always would come to me for advice. The girls always called me "Dick McLeod" in school. I never knew why, but that was the name for me. (as cited in McCluskey & Smith, 2001, p. 46)

In this regard, the underpinnings of Bethune's transformational leadership behavior(s) were about building trust and providing others with a role model that they sought to emulate (Bono & Judge, 2004; Simic, 1998; Stone, Russell, & Patterson, 2003). This idealized influence among her peer group commanded respect and admiration regardless of her race. Along with her leadership skills blossoming, the seed of her integrationist ideals also began to grow and cultivate. Her engagement with and influence over peers, teachers, and administrators became an impetus for inspiration and motivation to build cross racial coalitions to further her agenda of equality and full citizenship for Black Americans.

Foundation and Motivation

In 1894, Mary McLeod Bethune attended Dwight Moody's Institute for Home and Foreign Missions (now Moody Bible Institute) on yet another scholarship from Mary Crissman, the Quaker seamstress. She graduated and wanted to visit Africa on a mission. However, she was denied and told that Black missionaries were not needed. Nevertheless, she decided to teach and here the story of her leadership legacy unfolds.

Bethune's leadership legacy is multifaceted with her roles as educator, advocate, wife, mother, politician, intellectual, and pioneer. Her legacy speaks volumes as she learned from the best (such as Lucy Laney, Booker T. Washington) while also teaching others (such as Eleanor Roosevelt, Franklin D. Roosevelt, James Gamble, Thomas White, and John D. Rockefeller) about the plight of Black Americans in conjunction with winning them over as allies. Her transformational leadership qualities were apparent in that she recreated political connections with the alienated masses, but she also motivated those apathetic (Burns, 1978) to the plight of Black Americans.

After teaching at Haines Normal Institute from 1896 to 1904 (Hanson, 2003; McCluskey & Smith, 2001), founded by Lucy Laney, Bethune later moved to Daytona Beach, Florida where she started the Daytona Education and Industrial Institute for Negro girls. She had six students, five girls and her son Albert. She started the school with $1.50. They used blueberry juice for ink and charcoal and wood for pencils, items that were donated by local Black churches and businessmen. Occasionally, Bethune would go to the dump to find usable items to furnish her school.

Bethune's leadership for her school, which eventually became Bethune Cookman College, was a culmination of her vision, zeal, and strategic partnerships with wealthy Whites.

As a transformational leader, Bethune had an undying vision for the Daytona Institute for Girls. She foresaw the impact of her work generations ahead, while also realizing she would not live long enough to see the magnitude of her work. Her relationships with many White philanthropists and benefactors spoke highly to her ability to galvanize and motivate others in support of her vision. In this manner, Bethune encompassed the role of an inspirational motivator (Kelly, 2003). She used her charisma to motivate her students to meet high academic standards. But she also used charisma to motivate benefactors and future administrators to engulf themselves into the organization and live out her vision. For example, when seeking funding for her school, she met with James Gamble of Procter and Gamble at his home several times. In their initial meetings, she did not ask for monetary donations. Instead, she spoke of her vision to educate Black girls and the positive impact on society and industry. After courting Gamble, she asked him to be a "trustee of the vision" (Hanson, 2003; McCluskey & Smith, 2001). Being a trustee of the vision sparked an interest of the industrial changes Gamble was seeking. It must be noted that although White benefactors gave of their time and money to Black educational institutions, they also had ulterior motives to grow their companies by being supplied with a bountiful workforce. Bethune knowingly was aware of this motivating factor. However, she used this knowledge to her advantage in stimulating teamwork and creating synergy for cross racial coalitions that were taboo at the time. The alliances worked well for Bethune in helping Blacks receive education, job training, and in her mind, self-efficacy.

These strategic partnerships with Black intellectuals and White benefactors were transformational and transforming. They not only changed the lives of people, they forever changed the operation of institutions. This changing of the guard coincides with the revolutionary potential of transformational leadership. Through Mary McLeod Bethune's application of transformational leadership, she embodied radical reconstruction of schooling as espoused by Dantley (2003a). The structuring of integrated boards and wealthy benefactors by Mary McLeod Bethune was a radical move in the 19th and 20th centuries. Through this radical visioning, Daytona Normal School for girls' enrollment grew exponentially, and around 1907 a $5 down payment (total payment was $250) was used to purchase a tract of land that was being used as a dump (Smith, 2009; Rashid, 2009) on which to build a larger home for the school. In 1910, there were roughly 100 pupils with the value of the school buildings an estimated $100,000 (McCluskey & Smith, 2001). By 1923, the school merged with Cookman Institute for Men and the value of eight buildings was assessed at $250,000. Even through the Great Depression, the school was still able to function and meet Florida State educational standards. In 1914, the schools became Bethune Cookman College. She bragged of her school and said:

> We have fourteen modern buildings, a beautiful campus of thirty two acres, an enrollment in regular and summer sessions of 600 students, a faculty of thirty two, and 1,800 graduates. The college property, now valued at more than $800,000, is entirely unencumbered. (Bethune, 1972, p. 854)

Whether through written documents, motivational speeches, and/or conversations, Bethune inspired collaborators as well as giving them ownership in the fulfillment of the vision. This transformational leadership behavior was inspirational motivation. She displayed a contagious level of optimism, enthusiasm, and hope in the future. In essence, she encouraged others to contribute to the development of the vision.

Bethune was president part time at Bethune Cookman College between 1936 and 1942. At the same time, she was also director of the National Youth Administration (NYA) under President Franklin D. Roosevelt (Hanson, 2003; McCluskey & Smith, 2001).

Public Intellectual and Womanist Traditions

Among her duties of building and growing her school, Mary McLeod Bethune became heavily involved in the women's club movement. The Black women's club movement emerged as a response to an increasing need for social programs in the Black community and to combat institutional forms of racism (Barnett, 1996). She joined the National Association of Colored Women (NACW) apparently to get support and publicity for her school (Collier-Thomas, 1993). Nevertheless, she emerged as a leader of women. In 1917, she became president of the Florida Federation of Colored Women. In 1920, she founded the Southeastern Federation of Colored Women. In 1924, she became the president of NACW. Throughout her fast trajectory in the women's club movement, she became disillusioned and concerned about the fragmentation or lack of consistent focus of local women's groups (Collier-Thomas, 1993). At the time, women's groups were vehicles to "raise money for male dominated organizations and male defined causes" (p. 854) in conjunction with the "lack of clear focus and commitment to women's issues and especially to working class and poor Black women" (p. 854).

In 1934, she founded the National Council of Negro Women (NCNW). This women's club was a successful attempt to galvanize and streamline efforts on the behalf of Black women. Prior to the formation of the NCNW, many of the clubs operated independently of each other or were affiliated through White women's clubs (McCluskey & Smith, 2001). The NCNW was structured to permit "all national bodies of women, young and old, to pool their thinking and all together speak as one voice and mind for the highest good of the race" (McCluskey & Smith, 2001). The NCNW published a newsletter, *Telefact*, and a journal titled the *AfraAmerican Women's Journal*. These publications mobilized more than a million Black women for social justice causes at the national level for the first time in United States history (Barnett, 1996). Under Bethune's command the Council, as NCNW was often called, leadership evolved.

The Council (NCNW) developed and formed local chapters to stimulate the grassroots power base. One of the goals of NCNW was to win allies among mainstream society. They also tackled White women's organizational hegemony (McCluskey & Smith, 2001). Through her political connections with Eleanor Roosevelt, Bethune's influence and leadership would impact Black women by lobbying for policies and employment that favored Black people in general and Black women in particular. In 1938, the NCNW hosted a White House conference on Negro Women and Children showcasing the role Black women play in democracy. In 1940, Bethune publicly petitioned the president for administrative jobs in national defense for Black women. The following year she protested the exclusion of Black women from the National Women's Advisory Council on soldiers' welfare (Hanson, 2003; McCluskey & Smith, 2001). During her tenure as NCNW president, Bethune vocalized her disdain between WWII and democracy. She vehemently opposed and spoke of the hypocrisy of American democracy that almost always excluded Black Americans. While under the leadership of Bethune, NCNW was able to get Black women into military officer roles in the Women's Army Corps during WWII. She stated in her writings as NCNW president, "you and I must fight as never before to make our government realize the ideals upon which it was founded" (McCluskey & Smith, 2001).

As Bethune emerged as a leader of women, an aspect of her transformational leadership ability that blossomed was that of public intellectual, and she fostered intellectual stimulation (Bono & Judge, 2004; Simic, 1998) among her staff, collaborators, and/or benefactors. Cornel West (1999) argued that an intellectual articulates a truth that frees suffering to speak (as cited in Dantley & Tillman, 2010). He further posited that a public intellectual "creates a vision of the world that puts into limelight the social misery that is usually hidden or concealed by dominant viewpoints of society (West, 1999, p. 551).

In line with Bono and Judge (2004) and Kelly (2003), a transformational leader is also one who provides intellectual stimulation by changing their awareness of existing problems and their capacity to solve problems. By doing this, Bethune questioned assumptions about democracy, education, and Black women's role in emancipation for the Black community. Her fearless questioning and critique of the status quo empowered those under her influence to do the same. She had influence in many spheres and circles. She used her position as NCNW President, College President, and political friendships to voice the suffrage of Black people. Many refer to her as feminist in the traditional sense, but in her application of leadership she clearly demonstrated the elements of womanism, which is defined as a consciousness that incorporates racial, cultural, national, economic, and political considerations (Walker, 1983). In doing so, Bethune was very clear about her intentions and where Black women fit into the fight for equality and full citizenship for Black Americans. She shared Lucy Laney's notion that educated Black women should assume the "burden" to uplift their race by providing moral leadership at home and in the community. Her lifelong commitment to improving the economic and political clout of Black women exemplified this belief (McCluskey & Smith, 2001).

In her speech "Closed Doors," Bethune attempted to speak to the consciousness of white America as her audience was mostly white northerners. She spoke of the ills created by systemic racism. She stated:

> Not only the cultural avenues, but the economic fields are closed also...The white collar jobs are largely closed to the majority of Negroes although they have given themselves to the making of this country...the doors in almost every field–political, educational, economical, and social are closed, barred against him, but they must be opened. Shall it be a question whether or not the Negro, himself, will batter down the doors; whether or not the government will open some of them; whether or not the fair mindedness of the country shall force them to open is a question...Theoretically, to be an American citizen implies that every American citizen shall have life, liberty, and pursuit of happiness without anyone else's hindrance. Yet these rules do not apply equally to the Negro as the White man...Whether it be my religion, my aesthetic taste, my economic opportunity, my educational desire, whatever the craving is, I find a limitation because I suffer the greatest known

handicap, a Negro–a Negro woman. (Bethune as cited in McCluskey & Smith, 2001, pp. 15-16)

Bethune's role as womanist (perspective and experience as a woman of color (Walker, 1983), and public intellectual engaged her audience in a diplomatic tone, yet she never wavered in her goal of economic, educational, and political emancipation from de facto and de jure racism. She was a genius in her ability to speak boldly about racism and used a fertile metaphor of a "closed door" for civil rights. As a transformational leader, Bethune recognized that in order to confront closed doors, she needed tact, skill, and persistence to open other doors. Her intellect, political intuitiveness, and cross racial alliances helped her achieve her goals.

Transformational Leadership Praxis

Bethune continued to use her political connections to gain economic and educational progress for Black Americans. She was appointed Director of the Division of Negro Affairs (also referred to as the Black Cabinet) and was the first Black woman to head a federal agency. She was responsible for releasing federal funds to help Blacks matriculate through school based programs. She was the only Black agent releasing funds. She made sure Black educational institutions participated in the Civilian Pilot Training Program which was one of the first to graduate Black pilots (Hanson, 2003; McCluskey & Smith, 2001). Bethune used her position as Director to advocate for the appointment of Black officials to positions of political power. She was ahead of her time, a visionary. In her worldview, she believed that Black women were better suited to negotiate with whites than Black men and were therefore largely responsible for Black advancement (Hanson, 2003). Black women such as Mary McLeod Bethune continue to lead in the midst of the multiple intersections of oppression such as race, class, and gender. Black women developed strategies and institutions to help progress the race. Bethune's transformational leadership praxis incorporated her intellect, zeal, political savvy to, and undying belief in full citizenship for Blacks. In her essay

"Certain Unalienable Rights," she fervently stressed the importance of challenging the status quo of white supremacy (McCluskey & Smith, 2001). She stated:

> We must challenge, skillfully but resolutely, every sign of restriction or limit on our full American citizenship. We must seek every opportunity to place the burden of responsibility upon him who denies it. We should therefore, protest openly everything in the newspapers, on the radio, in the movies that smacks of discrimination and slander. (p. 41)

But even as she stated such, she sought interracial alliances and coalitions. At the time, her interracial alliances caused tension among Black and White leadership circles. Bethune had a vision of Black self-empowerment. Her leadership praxis was strategic and politically savvy, a testament to her commitment to Black success. She insisted that her primary interest would be the plight of the masses of Black folk and sought to achieve the goal(s) by any means necessary. To some she is seen as opportunistic, but to others she merely exercised her keen political skills. Aubrey Williams, a White southerner who worked with Bethune in the National Youth Administration under President Roosevelt described her in this manner:

> She was a damn good politician. She knew how to use other people to get what she wanted to achieve. She never played the losers. She played the winners. She made the republicans her friends when they were in power; she made the democrats her friends when they were in power. She had good goals. There was nothing small about them, and she used any means at hand to achieve them. (Martin, 1956 as cited in McCluskey & Smith, 2001, p. 62)

Bethune's leadership was encompassing of multiple agendas and strategies. She had her own brand of pragmatic idealism (McCluskey & Smith, 2001) which called for education associated with Black empowerment. She never relinquished the ideal of achieving total integration or full citizenship of Blacks into American life. In so doing, she also recognized and fought for Black stewardship of Black institutions (Hanson, 2003). She never wavered in her convictions, but she adjusted her approach.

Bethune's leadership legacy provides some insight into the racial politics of her time (Hanson, 2003).

The Bethune Legacy

Bethune was a transformational leader as well as a strategist. It is widely known that she wore multiple hats and was successful in many of her endeavors. According to Channing Tobias, Bethune was courageous yet cautious in her leadership efforts. She had the ability to know when to publicly challenge systemic racism and when to press towards her agenda in tempered movements. Her transformational qualities were a source of empowerment for many especially those students that would leave Bethune Cookman College to positively impact their local communities. However, there is a side of Bethune's leadership that is rarely discussed. As some scholars have noted, such as E. Franklin Frazier, that as Bethune rose to power she developed an "ego problem" that prevented self-reflection and self-criticism, which is a major pitfall of any transformational leader. Yet and still, she managed to hold onto her core beliefs of religious faith, racial pride, and equal opportunity for Black women and men in America. Bethune was supportive of those that promoted her vision. Through written documents, we get to see a demanding side of Bethune. Her reputation, that of the school, and perceived unity among administrators was of extreme importance.

Because of her varied positions in the public and civic arenas, Bethune began to delegate duties of running the school/college to others. Dr. Abram L. Simpson was personally hired by Bethune to advance the school's academic content. He was employed for two years. In 1938, during an interview, he publicly questioned Bethune's curriculum decisions and stated his belief that too much emphasis was put on college prep classes instead of the industrial arts (Hanson, 2003). Simpson made two grave errors; he publicly questioned Bethune's vision and the academic integrity of the institution. Bethune, known for her political savvy, was concerned that this interview would have a negative impact on the reputation of the school and her ability to raise operating and development funds. In a letter written to Simpson about his dismissal, Bethune stated:

> Your coming to Bethune Cookman College was my own dream and request, and certainly no one would be more eager for your success than I. I have given careful study to your administrative ability as it has been reflected in the institution to your business ability as you have followed through the business program of the school. I have found, through unbiased study, that your administrative ability, your business follow up and your ability to check on the details of the schools operation, do not fit into the pattern of this institution. They do not indicate you are the person we are seeking here. (Hanson, 2003, p. 85)

In his dismissal, Bethune praised his intellectual ability and leadership potential. We suspect she had to make an executive decision about the future of the school. Some scholars have noted that her inability to relinquish control caused administrators such as Simpson to be frustrated with operating the school in her absence.

James Colston served as president of Bethune Cookman between 1942 and 1946. He also endured criticism during this time. Some scholars suggest that Bethune was harshest on her male employees, especially when they questioned or changed curriculum or funding sources. Bethune made it very clear that her vision for Bethune Cookman College, her vision was the rule. She was not the president and stepped down from her post in name only. She involved herself in the daily operation of the school. In other words, when it came to her vision, she could micromanage the execution of her vision. As seen with Simpson, she dismissed anyone who she felt did not align with her vision.

By no means was Bethune a perfect leader; after all she was human. She possessed many transformational leadership qualities, but she also lacked the ability to let go and trust others to interpret and grow her vision. However, we cannot deny the fact that Mary McLeod Bethune was a transformational leader. She critiqued systemic injustice, raised the level of awareness and consciousness of those working with her, and most importantly, she changed people's lives, and transformed institutions and organizations.

In summary, Bethune was always preoccupied with her leadership legacy. In 1955, she wrote a letter to *Ebony* magazine. It was a passing of the baton to the next generation urging them to love one another, have hope in the future, develop confidence in each other, desire education, respect power, have faith in God, be prideful in being Black, desire to live peacefully with others, and be good stewards over the lives of young people. Her message was prophetic as she was urging the generation after her to serve and continue fighting for equality. Bethune lived for her vision and died wanting others to continue the vision.

Herstory–Shirley Chisholm: An Unbought and Unbossed Catalyst for Change

I want history to remember me not just as the first Black woman to be elected to Congress, not as the first Black woman to have made a bid for the presidency of the United States, but as a Black woman who lived in the 20th century and dared to be herself. I want to be remembered as a catalyst for change in America. (Shirley Chisholm in a 2004 interview with Donna Brazile)

Transformational leaders hold values and work toward the common good. Thus, they help followers satisfy as many of their individual human needs (safety, shelter, food) as possible as they move to higher order needs (e.g. to love, to learn, and to leave a legacy). Barbuto (2005) noted that they engender trust, admiration, loyalty, and respect amongst their followers. It is said to involve leaders and followers raising one another's achievements, morality, and motivations to levels that might otherwise have been impossible (Barnett, 2003; Chekwa, 2001; Crawford, Gould & Scott, 2003; Southwest Educational Development Laboratory, 2004). This description of a transformational leader quite aptly describes Congresswoman Shirley Chisholm.

Shirley Anita St. Hill was born to working class immigrant parents of West Indian heritage in Brooklyn, NY on November 30, 1924. As such, she had an early connection to and respect for understanding hard work and providing for the basic human needs. In 1928, at the tender age of three, she (along with her two sisters) was taken by her mother to Barbados to live with her maternal grandmother, Mrs. Emily Seale. After a nine-day voyage on the Atlantic Ocean via the *Vulcania*, they arrived in Barbados to live on a farm. While her mother returned to the states, she and her sisters (as well as cousins) would reside in Barbados for seven more years. As Chisholm noted about her grandmother, "She always told me, 'Stand up and be counted,' I would come home from school and she would say, 'Stand up, girl. Keep your head up. Approach me like you know where you're going.' She instilled in me my personality" (Clift & Brazaitis, 2000, p. xxiii). This time in Barbados would lay the foundation for who she would become in life, both personally and professionally, as well as begin the formation of the legacy that she would someday leave to the world.

Ordinary Yet Charismatic Grace: Idealized Influence

Transformational leaders must have the ability to influence others with their inspirational qualities. Avolio, Waldman, and Yammarino's (1991) concept of "idealized influence" involves leaders being admired and respected, and followers wanting to emulate them. Shirley Chisholm was a charismatic leader. Yukl (2009) noted that the attributes of a charismatic leader include a personal magnetism, a dramatic, persuasive manner of speaking, strong enthusiasm, and strong convictions. She had an ordinary yet charismatic grace. She was one of the people, though, with star quality. She began her career in education as a nursery school teacher and in 1972 made a run for the Office of President of the United States. Her ordinariness was attractive. In her memoir, *Unbought and Unbossed*, she described herself as a regular lady, not very different from all the other women who lived in her Bedford-Stuyvesant, Brooklyn neighborhood. These women were raised to be respectable, hardworking, and possess a strong religious core. Yet, there was something about her.

Charisma is defined as a rare trait found in certain human personalities usually including extreme charm and a magnetic quality of personality and/or appearance along with innate and powerfully sophisticated personal communicability and persuasiveness. Shirley Chisholm's honesty and her convictions were a breath of fresh air in the New York political machine, as well as the U.S. Congress. Her refusal in the face of tremendous odds to not accept the status quo was an attractive quality. Her use of emphatic tone and repetition inspired followers, particularly women. She challenged the long-held stereotypes of women that all we were good for was cleaning and child rearing. She reconstituted this view in the realm of politics, saying that women would "clean up" a corrupt system (Brown, 2008, p. 1019). She was admired, loved, and respected by the "everyday" people. She embodied Laubach's (2007) definition of charisma:

> People naturally like to be around people who are pleasant, joyful and smiling. It is a natural response to a natural trait of influential people who are great at attracting others. Call it charisma if you want. I prefer to call it care-isma. It demonstrates you care about your attitude, you care about the influence you have on others, and you care about others.

Chisholm cared. She cared about people, she cared about causes, and she cared about country. She was genuine in her caring. Although she was a strong opponent of racism and held liberal views, that did not stop her from reaching across the aisle to her more conservative colleagues. For example when one of her opponents for the Democratic nomination, Alabama Gov. George Wallace, was the victim of an assassination attempt that left him paralyzed, she visited him in the hospital and was criticized in the Black community. She said that when Wallace saw her, he asked, "What are your people going to say?" Her answer to him was, "I know what they're going to say. But I wouldn't want what happened to you to happen to anyone."

Another aspect of Chisholm's charismatic grace was her "style." From her physical presentation of self to her campaign style, she balanced it all with grace. Brown (2008) aptly noted, "Chisholm's clothing, accessories, and demeanor conveyed her betwixt and between cultural identity and marked her as a participant in a unique moment in American political history" (p. 1021). She was an irresistible force. Additionally, in capitalizing on her personal campaign style, she noted, "I have a way of talking that does something to people. I have a theory about campaigning. You have to let them feel you" (Brownmiller, 1969). In the late '60s and early '70s, she represented a cutting edge style of leadership; she was bold and solid in her demeanor and character. As the first Black woman to ever be elected to Congress in 1968, Shirley Chisholm added a new perspective and new view of political leadership. She advocated for an activist government to redress economic, social, and political injustices. In her 1972 bid to become the Democratic Party candidate for the U.S. presidency, she declared, "My presence before you now symbolizes a new era in American political history...Americans all over are demanding a new sensibility and new philosophy."

As a charismatic leader, she used her position and voice to bring attention to marginalized groups and varying inequalities. She made manifest House's (1977, as cited in Yukl, 2009) view of charismatic leadership in that:

- She was self-confident and held strong convictions;
- She was competent and successful;
- She articulated ideological goals that were rooted in her followers' values, ideals and aspirations;
- She set an example in her behavior for others to imitate; and
- She communicated high expectations for herself, others, and her country.

She was, as noted by Brown (2008), "a smart, mature, and politically savvy woman" (p. 1021).

Yes We Can: Inspirational Motivation

Before President Barack Obama ever used as his slogan "Yes We Can," Shirley Chisholm has already *done so* and invited, challenged, and welcomed folks along with her on the journey. Avolio et al., (1991) noted that those leaders who identify with the second "I" are those who inspire those around them by providing meaning and challenge. Chisholm's own motivation emanated from her familial background and upbringing. Because of her own immigrant identity and her family's working-class background, she felt an impetus to succeed. This resonated with those followers and supporters who too strived for success and had come from where she did. Kouzes and Posner (2008) noted that successful leaders don't try to push people; instead, they invite people to join in the adventure, and they provide further choices along the way. Chisholm inhabited a unique historical moment that motivated progressive citizens to embrace her "crossroads" status, i.e., the intersection of race, class, gender, and immigrant status (Brown, 2008, p. 1015).

Covey (2000) noted that motivating followers requires the successful leader to listen within the frame of reference to others. Chisholm's message resonated with the people. She also recognized that being female and being sensitive to gendered concerns was an advantage (Gallagher, 2007). For example, in working with the "Key Women of America" group, she built a strong base wherein they solidly backed her candidacy in 1964 and she was able to win the election to the New York State Assembly. Because of her continued loyalty to her word and to the people, while she had to run for her assembly seat three times in four years (due to reapportionment), she won each time and was still as committed to her constituents as they were to her. She noted in an interview with the *Amsterdam News* (1966), "I really feel like that so long as I fight for the people, I have nothing to worry about."

Chisholm's own motivation was solidly grounded and established from her birth. She noted in a 1968 interview that "from the time I was two my mother said I was born to lead" (Gallagher, 2007, p. 397). Watching her parents deal with their economic challenges as well as the West Indian values that undergirded their lives, she greatly desired to succeed. Her political passion and savvy were born out of her father's own passions. He had been a bakery assistant, a factory worker and a janitor; yet, he was a well-read man whom his oldest daughter idolized. He was a strong follower of Marcus Garvey (a Garveyite) and who she stated had "instilled a pride in ourselves and our race" (Chisholm, 1970, p. 14). Her parents and her heritage were role models for her, and she took her cues from that to model the way (Kouzes & Posner, 2008) for others. Also she took to heart the words of her grandmother, "Shirley, nothing can stop you if you are determined not to be distracted by temptation of the world. If you have strong character and determination and if you apply yourself, you will rise to the top" (Hicks, 1971, pp. 24-25). She was resourceful and self-sufficient. Because of her strong will, work, successes and failures, others have been able to stand on her shoulders in now these later years.

"I breathe fire": Intellectual Stimulation

Shirley Chisholm was often called "pepperpot" (West Indian stew made of meat, cinnamon, hot peppers, and other spices) as she was often quoted as saying, "I breathe fire." She breathed truth and coupled that with action. She was that rare combination of sweet, spicy, and smart, and she knew how to wield the power that came from this. She knew that her intellect was needed and that it was advantageous; yet she also knew that as a Black woman, it was not enough. She stated:

> I suffered from two obstacles—I was a Black person and I was a woman...I met far more discrimination as a woman in the field of politics. That was a revelation to me...They said I was an intellectual person, that I had the ability, but that this was no place for a woman. (Clift & Brazaitis, 2000, p. 28).

Avolio et al. (1991) noted that in this intellectual stimulation, creativity is encouraged and questioning assumptions and challenging new thinking is also encouraged. Regarding the development of her intellect, Chisholm (1970, 2010) believed that her time in Barbados laid the foundation for her later life. On her early schooling in Barbados, she reflected, "Years later I would know what an important gift my parents had given me by seeing to it that I had my early education in the strict, traditional British-style schools of Barbados. If I speak and write easily now, that early education is the main reason" (Chisholm, 2010, p. 27). It was this cultural heritage that developed and influenced her both intellectually and politically.

This intellectual stimulation was honored and fertilized in her home as she grew up. Daily during family dinner time, her father would ask his daughters what they learned in school on that day. According to Chisholm (2010), it was not an idle question as his theme was:

> You must make something of yourselves. You've got to go to school, and I'm not sending you to play either. Study and make something of yourselves. Remember, only the strong people survive in this world. God gave you a brain; use it. (p. 33)

Though she received several scholarships, after graduating from Brooklyn's Girls' High, she matriculated onto Brooklyn College. Tuition was free and she could still live at home to save on room and board. While in college, from where she graduated *cum laude*, she honed her public speaking skills as a member of the Debate Society. While she may have had a pronounced lisp, it did not prevent her from being one of the more forceful speakers of the 20th century. Gutgold (2006) noted that there was no flowery language or indirect references in her speeches. In the now famous 1969 speech in support of the Equal Rights Amendment, she stated:

> This is what it comes down to: artificial distinctions between persons must be wiped out of the law. Legal discrimination between the sexes is, in almost every instance, founded on outmoded views of society and the pre-scientific beliefs about psychology and physiology. It is time to sweep away these relics of the past and set further generations free of them.

When she spoke, she was very clear about what she meant and she was always up for a good fight.

The Good Fight: Individualized Consideration

> I stand before you today as a candidate for the Democratic nomination for the Presidency of the United States. I am not the candidate of Black America, although I am Black and proud. I am not the candidate of the

women's movement of this country, although I am a woman, and I am
equally proud of that. I am not the candidate of any political bosses or
special interests. I am the candidate of the people. (Chisholm, 1972)

Individualized consideration requires that leaders give special
attention to each follower's needs in order to cultivate growth.
According to Homrig (2001) individual consideration treats each
follower as an individual and provides coaching, mentoring and
growth opportunities. It is in this approach where there is not only
education of the next generation of leaders, but it also fulfills the
individual's need for self-actualization, self-fulfillment, and self-
worth. It also naturally propels followers to further achievement
and growth.

Shirley Chisholm managed to fulfill this role as
transformational leader by being a tempered radical, staying in
the system to fight. While she went against the pulse of the time,
which was a radical resistance to the system, she believed in the
promise of the political structure and knew there was much to be
changed, but she had to be a part of it to make change happen
(Gallagher, 2007). In truly understanding her role, her mission,
and her vision as a part of the political infrastructure, she
emphatically noted as she referred to those who placed her in
office:

I'm fighting. I tell them. I know that I'm in Congress, but you can see I
haven't started to conform. I haven't sold out. I'm fighting within the
system. There is no other place to fight, if you only understood it. There's
no other way for us to survive because we really don't have anything.
(Chisholm, 1973 as cited in McCartney, 1993, p. 117)

Chisholm believed in serving the people at the micro-level as
well as the macro-level. In a reflection about her candidacy for the
presidency, she noted that it accomplished one thing, "The next
time a woman of whatever color, or a dark-skinned person
whatever sex aspires to be President, the way should be a little
smoother because I helped pave it" (Chisholm, 1973, p. 151).

The success of her "Unbought and Unbossed" campaign was
attributed both to widespread support from women as well as her
ability to address Puerto Rican voters in Spanish (she had majored

in Spanish at Brooklyn College). Chisholm spoke Spanish fluently and used that as a personal, individual consideration to connect with her constituents and potential supporters. Chisholm explained why she ran for president:

> I ran for the presidency, despite hopeless odds, to demonstrate the sheer will and refusal to accept the status quo....The next time a woman runs, or a Black, a Jew or anyone from a group that the country is 'not ready' to elect to its highest office, I believe that he or she will be taken seriously from the start. (Chisholm, 1973, p. 152)

With this sense of duty and citizenship, she was the embodiment of an ethic of care and an ethic of justice–a combination of compassion and fairness (Siddle Walker, & Snarey, 2004). She genuinely cared for and about those among whom she lived amongst. Her stance was not a stereotypical politician's stance just to be elected. She recognized and accepted the challenge of her purpose as a transformational leader, a real catalyst for change.

As an assemblywoman from 1964 to 1968, she spearheaded legislation providing for state-funded day care centers and for unemployment insurance for domestic workers. Connecting to her passion for education and her vocation as a teacher, there were many bills that she shepherded through the Education Committee. One major accomplishment was a financial aid program, Search for Elevation, Education and Knowledge (SEEK). Passed into law in 1965, SEEK reached out to students of color who lacked the necessary academic requirements to enter state universities by providing them with scholarships and remedial training. Other legislative successes included boosting school spending limits as well as wiping out the practice of stripping tenure from women teachers who took maternity leave.

Other work that was completed while in the New York State Assembly included proposing legislation to eliminate racial discrimination in banking, investments, and insurance practices. She was also to have passed into law a requirement for city police to complete training in civil rights issues. For the economically disadvantaged, she advocated for more affordable public housing (Gallagher, 2007).

On the national level she also worked to advance the goal of racial equality. In 1969 her first statement as a Congresswoman before the United States House of Representatives reflected her commitment to prioritizing the needs of the disadvantaged, especially children: She proclaimed her intention to vote "no" on every money bill that came to the floor of the house that provided any funds for the Department of Defense. She supported programs that provided housing and education aid to cities, voted to uphold laws that would end discrimination in federally funded jobs, and promoted new antidiscrimination legislation. Abortion rights also became a focal point in her politics. She was one of the first African American women to have a pro-choice stance on the issue of abortion and she supported legalized abortions. In "Facing the Abortion Question," she argued the importance of Black women's ability to get safe, legal abortions, while being especially sensitive to the plight of poor women who had been more negatively impacted by unwanted pregnancies (Chisholm, 1973).

Chisholm wasted little time in displaying her outspokenness and fearlessness when she challenged the House's seniority system after being placed on the Agriculture Committee, a slot that did little for her urban district. She demanded reassignment and was given a seat on the Veteran Affairs Committee. She recalled this challenging of the system:

> Every time I rose, two or three men jumped up...Men were smiling and nudging each other as I stood there trying to get the floor. After six or seven attempts, I walked down an aisle to the "well," the open space between the front row of seats and the Speaker's dais, and stood there. I was half afraid and half enjoying the situation, as Mr. Mills, who was the chair, conferred with the majority leader, Carl Albert of Oklahoma..."For what purpose is the gentlewoman from New York standing in the well?" Mr. Mills asked. "I'd been trying to get recognized for half an hour, Mr. Chairman, but evidently you were unable to see me, so I came down to the well. I would just like to tell the caucus why I vehemently reject my committee assignment. (Chisholm, 2010, p. 100)

The seniority she earned over seven terms (as the only woman on the House Rules Committee) made her effective in building coalitions among liberal politicians, yet she was not afraid to cross the aisle to work with and support her much more conservative colleagues. In addition to supporting women's equality, she was instrumental in advancing welfare legislation designed to help poor and needy citizens. Not afraid of the fight and standing on her beliefs, she diligently advocated for the rights of women and people of color and was a fierce opponent of the Vietnam War. She was unequivocal in her beliefs in spite of what the popular opinion may have been at the time.

"Veni, vidi, vici": Fulfilling the Leadership Challenge

The legacy of Shirley Anita St. Hill Chisholm is that she fulfilled and surpassed the leadership challenge as purported by Kouzes and Posner (1995, 2008). Her one goal was to be a catalyst for change. Her grandmother's early advice on success resonated through her life: "...nothing can stop you if you're determined not to be distracted by the world of temptation...If you have strong character and determination, and if you apply yourself, you will rise to the top" (Hicks, 1971, pp. 24-25). In actualizing her mission, she matched both the practice and the commitments that Kouzes and Posner (1995, 2008) identified for successful leadership:

> *Practice: Challenging the Process*
> Commitments:
> - Search out challenging opportunities to change, grow, innovate, and improve.
> - Experiment, take risks, and learn from the accompanying mistakes.
>
> *Practice: Inspiring a Shared Vision*
> Commitments:
> - Envision an uplifting and ennobling future
> - Enlist others in a common vision by appealing to their values, interests, hopes and dreams.
>
> *Practice: Enabling Others to Act*
> Commitments:
> - Foster collaboration by promoting cooperative goals and building trust.

- Strengthen people by giving power away, providing choice, developing competence, and assigning critical tasks.

Practice: Modeling the Way

Commitments:

- Set the example by behaving in ways that are consistent with shared values.
- Achieve small wins that promote consistent progress and build commitment.

Practice: Encouraging the Heart

Commitments:

- Recognize individual contributions to the success of every project.
- Celebrate team accomplishments regularly.

Chisholm's focus was simply on "the people." She not only fulfilled the "leadership challenge," but she also exemplified "resonant leadership" as articulated by Boyatzis and McKee (2005). Chisholm stepped up, charted a path through unfamiliar territory, and inspired people. She was indeed a great leader who was "awake, aware, and attuned...emotionally intelligent...face[d] sacrifice, difficulties, and challenges with empathy and compassion" for the people that she served (Boyatzis & McKee, 2005, p. 3). She articulated her identity as a feminist, as a Black American, and as a progressive politician and human being who was committed to improving the plight of the everyday working-class American of any and all races and cultural background (Brown, 2008). She was committed to rebuilding a "strong and just society" (Gallagher, 2007, p. 407). Her legacy for future leaders who want to walk in her footsteps as fighters and catalysts for change:

> I always tell people, I say, look, whatever goal you have in mind for yourself, pursue it. And never, never give up. You must look only to God and to your conscience for approval, not man. Because if you look to man, you'll always be mixed up and twisted....(Chisholm, 2010, p. 199)

Points to Consider

1. Antonakis and House (2002) stated, "leaders who provide customized socio-economic support to followers, while

developing and empowering them. This outcome is achieved by coaching and counseling followers, maintaining frequent contact with them, and helping them to self-actualize" (pp. 9-10). How is this approach different from what we see and experience from leaders today? What has changed?

2. Burns conceptualized that leadership as a moral endeavor was a fairly new concept. However, from the examples of the women in this text, this seems not to be the case. Why does it seem as if there isn't a delineation of spirituality from leadership in the Black woman's leadership praxis?

3. Why does the notion of spiritual leadership or spiritually infused leadership seem as a new concept to some and not others?

4. Mary McLeod Bethune was a resource for helping many in her community reconcile their bookkeeping and debts with the landowners; including poor Whites. What value if any can one gather from these alliances that crossed racial and class social systems?

5. Racial and class structures not only affected Blacks, but also affected the lives of poor whites. In your opinion, what complications were there when poor whites went to Blacks for help? How did this dynamic affect the social structures at the time?

6. Discuss the complexities of having competing social roles of mother, educator, wife, and advocate/humanitarian in a context where women were devalued and being Black was taboo? Discuss the implications of the intersections of race, class, and gender? How do intersections affect Black women differently?

7. What can be learned from Bethune and Chisholm's example of womanhood? Leadership? Visionary? Humanitarian?

8. What is the legacy of Chisholm's "Unbought and Unbossed" slogan? Is it still relevant for leadership in the 21st century?

9. What is the burden of being the "first" in relation to leadership? The promise? The legacy?

Suggested Readings

Barnett, E. (1996). Mary McLeod Bethune: Feminist, educator, and activist. In J. A. Banks & C. A. M. Banks (Eds.), *Multicultural education: Transformative knowledge and action*. Danvers, MA: Teachers College Press.

Barnwell, C. A. (2002). *The dialogics of self in the autobiographies of African-American public women: Ida B. Wells, Shirley Chisholm, Angela Davis and Anita Hill*. Ph.D. dissertation, Howard University, United States–District of Columbia. Retrieved December 20, 2010, from Dissertations & Theses: A&I. (Publication No. AAT 3085405).

Bass, B. M., & Riggio, R. E. (2006). *Transformational leadership*. Mahwah, NJ: Lawrence Erlbaum.

Bass, B. M., & Steidlmeier, P. "Ethics, character, and authentic transformational leadership behavior." *Leadership Quarterly*. v. 10 pp. 181-218.

Bethune, M. M. (1972). A college on a garbage dump. In G. Lerner (Ed.), *Black women in white America: A documentary history* (pp. 134-143). New York: Random House.

Boyatzis, R. & McKee, A. (2005). *Resonant leadership: Renewing yourself and connecting with others through mindfulness, hope, and compassion*. Boston: Harvard Business School Press.

Brown, T. L. (2008). "A new era in American politics": Shirley Chisholm and the discourse of identity. *Callaloo, 31*(4), 1013-1025.

Burns, J. M. (1978). *Leadership*. New York: Harper & Row.

Canas, K. A. (2002). *Barbara Jordan, Shirley Chisholm, and Lani Guinier: Crafting identification through the rhetorical interbraiding of value*. Ph.D. dissertation, The University of Utah.

Chisholm, S. (1969, May). *Equal rights for women*. Speech presented to the U.S. Congress, Washington, DC.

Chisholm, S. (1970). *Unbought and unbossed*. Boston, MA: Houghton Mifflin.

Chisholm, S. (1972, January). *Speech to announce candidacy for the U.S. presidency*. New York.

Chisholm, S. (1973). *The good fight.* New York: HarperCollins.

Chisholm, S. (2010). *Unbought and unbossed.* (Expanded 40th Anniversary Edition). Washington, DC: Take Riot Media.

Clift, E., & Brazaitis, T. (2000). *Madam president: Shattering the last glass ceiling.* New York: Scribner.

Collier-Thomas, B. (1993). National Council of Negro Women. In D. C. Hine (Ed.), *Black women in America: An historical encyclopedia* (pp. 853-864). Brooklyn, NY: Carlson.

Collier-Thomas, B., & Franklin, V. P. (Eds.). (2001). *Sisters in the struggle: African American women in the civil rights-black power movement.* New York: New York University Press.

Dantley, M. E. (2003a). Critical spirituality: Enhancing transformative leadership through critical theory and African American prophetic spirituality. *International Journal of Leadership in Education, 6*(3), 3-17.

Dantley, M. E. (2005). African American spirituality and Cornel West's notions of prophetic pragmatism: Restructuring educational leadership in American schools. *Education Adminstration Quarterly, 41*(4), 651-674.

Eagly, A. H., Johannesen-Schmidt, M. C., & van Engen, M. L. (2003). Transformational, transactional, and laissez-Faire leadership styles. *Psychological Bulletin, 129*(4), 569-591.

Gallagher, J. (2007). Waging "the good fight": The political career of Shirley Chisholm, 1953-1982. *The Journal of African American History, 92*(3), 393-416.

Generett, G. G., & Jeffries, R. B. (Eds.). (2003). *Black women in the field: Experiences understanding ourselves and others through qualitative research.* Cresskill, NJ: Hampton Press.

Gutgold, N. D. (2006). *Paving the way for madam president.* Lanham, MD: Lexington Books.

Hall, E. *The power of one: Mary McLeod Bethune's legacy in leadership, learning, and service.* Ph.D. dissertation, Cardinal Stritch University, United States - Wisconsin.

Hanson, J. A. (1997). *The ties that bind: Mary McLeod Bethune and the political mobilization of African-American women.* Ph.D. dissertation, The University of Connecticut.

Hanson, J. A. (2003). *Mary McLeod Bethune and Black women's political activism*. Columbia, MO: University of Missouri Press.

Jordan, J. (1972). *Fannie Lou Hamer*. New York: Thomas Y. Crowell Company.

Kark, R. (2004). The transformational leader: Who is (s)he? A feminist perspective. *Journal of Organizational Change Management, 17*(2), 160-176.

Kouzes , J. M., & Posner, B. Z. (1995). *The leadership challenge* (1st Edition). San Francisco: Jossey-Bass.

Kouzes , J. M. ,& Posner, B. Z. (2008). *The leadership challenge* (4th Edition). San Francisco: Jossey-Bass.

Lerner, G. (1992). *Black women in White America: A documentary history*. New York: Vintage Books.

Loden, M. (1985), *Feminine leadership: Or how to succeed in business without being one of the boys*. New York: Time Books,

Manning, T. T. (2002). Gender, managerial level, transformational leadership and work satisfaction. *Women in Management Review, 17*(5), 207-216.

Martin, E. D. (1956). *Mary McLeod Bethune: A prototype of the rising consciousness of the American negro*. M.A., Northwestern University.

McCartney, J. (1993). *Black power ideologies*. Philadelphia, PA: Temple University Press.

McCluskey, A. T. (1991). *Mary McLeod Bethune and the education of Black girls in the South, 1904-1923*. Ph.D. dissertation, Indiana University.

McCluskey, A. T., & Smith, E. M. (Eds.). (2001). *Mary McLeod Bethune: Building a better world essays and selected documents*. Indianapolis: Indiana University Press.

Powell, G. N., Butterfield, D. A., & Bartol, K. M. (2008). Leader evaluations: A new female advantage? *Gender in Management: An International Journal, 23*(3), 156-174.

Siddle Walker, V. & Snarey, J. R. (Eds.). (2004). *Race-ing moral formation: African American perspectives on care and justice*. New York: Teachers College Press.

Smith, S. K. (2009). *Crazy faith: Ordinary people, extraordinary lives*. Valley Forge: PA: Judson Press.

Stone, A., Russell, R., & Patterson, K. (2003). Transformational versus servant leadership–A difference in leader focus. Paper presented at the Servant Leadership Roundtable at Regent University, Virginia Beach, VA, on Oct.16, 2003.

Tichy, N. M. & Devanna, M. A. (1986). *The transformational leader.* New York: John Wiley.

Trinidad, C., & Normore, A. H. (2005). Leadership and gender: A dangerous liaison? *Leadership & Organization Development Journal, 26*(7), 574-590.

Walker, A. (1983). *In search of our mother' s garden.* New York: Harcourt Publishers.

West, C. (1999). *The Cornel West reader.* New York: Civitas.

Williams, G. *A passion for social equality: Mary McLeod Bethune's race woman leadership and the New Deal.* Ph.D. dissertation, University of Illinois at Chicago.

Yukl, G. A. (2009). *Leadership in organizations* (7th edition). Englewood Cliffs, NJ: Prentice Hall.

Video Resources: Teaching/learning tools to be used as supplementary material to support and expand the given topic.

- *12 Angry Men* (1957) – featuring Henry Fonda, Lee J. Cobb, E.G. Marshall, and Jack Klugman
- *12 Angry Men* (1997) – featuring Jack Lemmon, Courtney B. Vance, George C. Scott, and Ossie Davis
- *An Extraordinary Woman, The Legacy of Mary McLeod Bethune:* http://newsone.com/obama/celebrate-44/news-one-staff/video-mary-mcleod-bethune/
- *Chisholm 72: Unbought and Unbossed* (2004) – PBS Video
- *Dead Poets Society* (1988) – featuring Robin Williams and Ethan Hawke
- *Five Leadership Competencies for Transformational Leadership*
  http://gaian.com/five_leadership_competencies.htm
- *Hoosiers* (1986) featuring Gene Hackman, Dennis Hopper, and Barbara Hershey

- *Glory* (1989) – featuring Denzel Washington and Matthew Broderick
- *Jerry Maguire* (1996) – featuring Tom Cruise, Cuba Gooding, Jr., and Renee Zellweger
- *Martin Luther King, Jr.* "I Have a Dream" http://video.google.com/videoplay?docid=1732754907698549493#docid=432551007277565829
- *Mary McLeod Bethune: Champion for Education:* http://www.tmwmedia.com/Black_american_experience.html
- *Mona Lisa Smile* (2003) – featuring Julia Roberts, Kirsten Dunst, and Julia Stiles
- *Remember the Titans* (2000) – featuring Denzel Washington, Will Patton, and Wood Harris.
- *Shawshank Redemption* (1994) – featuring Tim Robbins, Morgan Freeman, and Bob Gunton.
- *Shirley Chisholm: First Black Congresswoman:* http://www.tmwmedia.com/Black_american_experience.html

References

Amsterdam News (1966, November 12), p. 51.

Antonakis, J. ,& House, R. J. (2002). An analysis of the full-range leadership theory: The way forward. In B. J. Avolio & F. Yammarino (Eds). *Transformational and charismatic leadership: The road ahead.* (pp. 3-33). New York: Elsevier Science.

Avolio, B. J., Waldman, D. A., & Yammarino, F. J. (1991). The four I's of transformational leadership, *Journal of European Industrial Training,* 50-58.

Barbuto, J.E. (2005). Motivation and transactional, charismatic, and transformational leadership: A test of antecedents. *Journal of Leadership and Organizational Studies,* 11(4), 26-40.

Barnett, E. (1996). Mary McLeod Bethune: Feminist, Educator, and Activist. In J. A. Banks & C. A. M. Banks (Eds.),

Multicultural education: Transformative knowledge and action. Danvers, MA: Teachers College Press

Bass, B. M., Avolio, B. J., and Jung, D. I. (1995). *MLQ multifactor leadership questionnaire: Technical report.* Redwood City: Mind Garden.

Bass, B. M., & Avolio, B. J. (1994). *Improving organizational effectiveness through transformational leadership.* Thousand Oaks, CA: Sage Publications.

Bass, B. M., & Riggio, R. E. (2006). *Transformational leadership.* Mahwah, NJ: Lawrence Erlbaum.

Bethune, M. M. (1972). A college on a garbage dump. In G. Lerner (Ed.), *Black women in white America: A documentary history* (pp. 134-143). New York: Random House.

Boyatzis, R. & McKee, A. (2005). *Resonant leadership: Renewing yourself and connecting with others through mindfulness, hope, and compassion.* Boston: Harvard Business School Press.

Brown, T. L. (2008). "A new era in American politics": Shirley Chisholm and the discourse of identity. *Callaloo, 31*(4), 1013-1025.

Brownmiller, S. (13 Apr. 1969) "This is Fighting Shirley Chisholm." *New York Times Magazine,* 32-33.

Bono, J., & Judge, T. (2004). Personality and transformational and transactional leadership: A meta-analysis. *Journal of Applied Psychology. 89*(5), 901-910.

Bryman, A. (1992). *Charisma and leadership in organizations.* London: Sage Publications.

Burns, J. M. (1978). *Leadership.* New York: Harper & Row.

Burns, J. M. (1979). *Leadership.* New York: Harper Torch.

Carless, S. A. (1998). Gender differences in transformational leadership: An examination of superior, leader and subordinate perspectives. *Sex Roles, 39,* 887-902.

Chekwa, E. (2001, July 12-14). Searching for African American transformational leaders. Paper present at the Academy of Business and Administrative Sciences 4th International Conference, Quebec City, Canada.

Chisholm, S. (1969, May). *Equal rights for women.* Speech presented to the U.S. Congress, Washington, DC.

Chisholm, S. (1970). *Unbought and unbossed.* Boston, MA: Houghton Mifflin.

Chisholm, S. (1972, January). *Speech to announce candidacy for the U.S. presidency* New York.

Chisholm, S. (1973). *The good fight.* New York: HarperCollins.

Chisholm, S. (2010). *Unbought and unbossed.* (Expanded 40th Anniversary Edition). Washington, DC: Take Riot Media.

Clark, S. P. (1962). *Echo in my soul.* New York: E. P. Dutton & Co.

Clift, E. & Brazaitis, T. (2000). *Madam president: Shattering the last glass ceiling.* New York: Scribner.

Collier-Thomas, B. (1993). National Council of Negro Women. In D. C. Hine (Ed.), *Black women in America: An historical encyclopedia* (pp. 853-864). Brooklyn, NY: Carlson.

Collier-Thomas, B., & Franklin, V. P. (Eds.). (2001). *Sisters in the struggle: African American women in the civil rights-black power movement.* New York: New York University Press.

Conger, J. A. (1999). Charismatic and transformational leadership in organizations: an insider's perspective on these developing streams of research. *The Leadership Quarterly,* 10(2), pp. 145-170.

Covey, S. R. (2000). *The 7 habits of highly effective people.* Philadelphia, PA: Running Press.

Crawford, C., Gould, L., & Scott, R. (2003). Transformational leader as champion and techie: implications for leadership educators. *Journal of Leadership Education, 2*(1), pp. 1-12.

Dantley, M. E. (2003a). Critical spirituality: Enhancing transformative leadership through critical theory and African American prophetic spirituality. *International Journal of Leadership in Education, 6*(3), 3-17.

Dantley, M. E. (2003b). Purposive driven leadership: The spiritual imperative to guiding schools beyond high-stakes testing and minimum proficiency. *Education and Urban Society, 35*(3), 273-291.

Dantley, M. E. (2005). African American spirituality and Cornel West's notions of prophetic pragmatism: Restructuring educational leadership in American schools. *Education Adminstration Quarterly, 41*(4), 651-674.

Dantley, M. E., & Tillman, L. C. (2010). Social justice and moral transformative leadership. In C. Marshall & M. Olivia (Eds.), *Leadership for social justice: Making revolutions in education.* Boston, MA: Allyn & Bacon.

Downton, J. V. (1973). *Rebel leadership: Commitment and charisma in the revolutionary process.* New York: Free Press.

Gallagher, J. (2007). Waging "the good figh": The political career of Shirley Chisholm, 1953-1982. *The Journal of African American History, 92*(3), 393-416.

Generett, G. G., & Jeffries, R. B. (Eds.). (2003). *Black women in the field: Experiences understanding ourselves and others through qualitative research.* Cresskill, NJ: Hampton Press.

Gutgold, N. D. (2006). *Paving the way for madam president.* Lanham, MD: Lexington Books.

Hanson, J. A. (2003). *Mary McLeod Bethune and Black women's political activism.* Columbia, MO: University of Missouri Press.

Helgesen, S, (1990). *The female advantage: Women's way of leadership.* New York: Doubleday

Hicks, N. (1971). *The honorable Shirley Chisholm, congresswoman from Brooklyn.* New York: Lion Books.

Homrig, M. A. (2001). *Transformational leadership.* Retrieved from http://leadership.au.af.mil/documents/homrig.htm (2010, October 24).

Jordan, J. (1972). *Fannie Lou Hamer.* New York: Thomas Y. Crowell Company.

Judge, T. A., & Piccolo, R. F. (2004). Transformational and transactional leadership: a meta-analytic test of their relative validity. *Journal of Applied Psychology, 89*/5, pp. 755-768.

Kelly, M. L. (2003, January 1). Academic advisers as transformational leaders. *The Mentor.* Retrieved October 25, 2010, from http://www.psu.edu/dus/mentor/030101mk.htm

Kouzes, J. M., & Posner, B. Z. (2008). *The leadership challenge* (1st Edition). San Francisco: Jossey-Bass.

Kouzes, J. M., & Posner, B. Z. (2008). *The leadership challenge* (4th Edition). San Francisco: Jossey-Bass.

Laubach, R. (2007). *What do you mean by charisma?* Retrieved from http://www.leadquietly.com/2007/07/what-do-you-mean-by-charisma.html (2010, October 20).

Lewis, P. V. (1996). *Transformational leadership: A new model for total church involvement.* Nashville, TN: Broadman & Holman.

Loden, M. (1985), *Feminine leadership: Or how to succeed in business without being one of the boys.* New York: Time Books,

Lowe, K. B., & Gardner, W. L. (2001). Ten years of the *Leadership Quarterly*: Contributions and challenges for the future. *Leadership Quarterly, 11*(4), 459-514.

Martin, E. D. (1956). *Mary McLeod Bethune: A prototype of the rising consciousness of the American negro.* M.A., Northwestern University.

McCartney, .J. (1993). *Black power ideologies.* Philadelphia, PA: Temple University Press.

McClellan, P. (2006). *Wearing the mantle: Spirited Black male servant leaders reflect on their leadership journey.* (Unpublished doctoral dissertation). Bowling Green State University, Bowling Green, OH.

McCluskey, A. T., & Smith, E. M. (Eds.). (2001). *Mary McLeod Bethune: Building a better world essays and selected documents.* Indianapolis, IN: Indiana University Press.

Northouse, P. G. (2007). *Leadership: Theory and practice* (4th Edition.). Thousand Oaks, CA: Sage.

Siddle Walker, V., & Snarey, J. R. (Eds.). (2004). *Race-ing moral formation: African American perspectives on care and justice.* New York: Teachers College Press.

Simic, I. (1998). Transformational leadership—the key to successful management of transformational organizational changes. *Facta Universitas*, 1(6), pp. 49-55.

Smith, S. K. (2009). *Crazy faith: Ordinary people, extraordinary lives.* Valley Forge: PA: Judson Press.

Spreitzer, G. M., Perttula, K. H., & Xin, K. (2005). Traditionality matters: an examination of the effectiveness of transformational leadership in the United States and Taiwan. *Journal of Organizational Behavior, 26*, 205-227.

Stewart, C. F. (1999). *Black spirituality and Black consciousness: Soul force, culture, and freedom in the African American experience.* Trent, NJ: Africa World Press.

Stone, A., Russell, R., & Patterson, K. (2003). Transformational versus servant leadership–A difference in leader focus. Paper presented at the Servant Leadership Roundtable at Regent University, Virginia Beach, VA, on Oct.16, 2003.

Tichy, N. M., & Devanna, M. A. (1986). *The transformational leader.* New York: John Wiley.

Walker, A. (1983). *In search of our mother's garden.* New York: Harcourt.

Walker, A. (1984). *In search of our mother's gardens.* New York: Mariner Books.

West, C. (1999). *The Cornel West reader.* New York: Civitas.

Yammarino, F. J., Dubinsky, A. J., Comer, L. B, & Jolson, M. A. (1997), Women and transformational and contingent reward leadership: A multiple-levels-of-analysis perspective. *Academy of Management Journal, 40,* 205-222.

Yukl, G. A. (2009). *Leadership in Organizations* (7th Edition). Englewood Cliffs, NJ: Prentice Hall.

Tempered Radicalism and Social Justice: A Likely Duo

The ends you serve that are selfish will take you no further than yourself
but the ends you serve that are for all, in common, will take you into
eternity. — Marcus Garvey

There has been a recent abundance of theoretical and conceptual work in the area of social justice and leadership (Blackmore, 2002; Bogotch, 2002; Dantley, 2002; Furman & Gruenewald, 2004; Larson & Murtadha, 2002; MacKinnon, 2000; Marshall & Ward, 2004; Rapp, 2002; Shields, 2004). As a theoretical construct, social justice is informed by multidisciplinary inquiry that struggles to accommodate distinct ontological and epistemological foundations (Cambron-McCabe & McCarthy, 2005).

Leadership for social justice has been defined by many and in many ways. For the purposes of this text, we will focus on two particular definitions. Theoharis (2007) defined it as the ways in which leaders make issues of race, class, gender, disability, sexual orientation, and other historically and currently marginalizing conditions in the United States central to their advocacy, leadership practice, and vision. Concomitantly, Dantley and Tillman (2006) noted that leadership for social justice investigates and poses solutions for issues that generate and reproduce societal inequities. Further, they go on to say that leadership for social justice interrogates the policies and procedures that shape organizations while they simultaneously perpetuate social inequalities and marginalization due to race, class, gender, and other markers of otherness. Of particular interest for this chapter is leadership for social justice in the realm of racism, sexism, and heterosexism as it relates to women of African descent and their devotion and activism to be change agents. Upon this foundation of social justice leadership, this chapter will layer feminism, Black feminist thought, and tempered radicalism to explore the lives of Audre Lorde and Barbara Jordan as purveyors of truth and standard setting legacies of social justice. Born just two years apart, they shared birth order, public and private identities, and life experiences, though each made her journey in very different ways.

Feminism and Leadership

Feminist methodology begins with the view that women are oppressed (Adler, Laney, & Packer, 1993). A review of the chronology of feminist research reveals that the first wave of early feminist theory focused on the struggle for the right to be educated. The second wave focused on the struggle for additional goals related to education: the right to criticize the accepted body of knowledge, the right to create knowledge, and the right to be educators and leaders (Reinharz, 1992). Klein (1983) argued that a fair amount of feminist scholarship has not contributed to women's visibility in a feminist frame of reference, but instead continues to perpetuate the dominant androcentric one. Thus, it has been "research *on* women rather than research *for* women. Research *for* women is that which tries to take women's needs, interests, and experiences into account and aims at being instrumental in improving women's lives in one or another..." (p. 90).

Shakeshaft (1989) developed several theoretical framework approaches for studying women in leadership positions. The symbolic interaction framework addressed how organizations (in particular schools) appear to women who administer them; a feminist framework which focuses on female leadership as community building; and a revisionist approach that addresses rethinking organization theory by adding women's experiences. However, simply adding women and stirring does not solve the problem. Specifically in the discipline of education, feminist theory has promoted a de-emphasis on dualism or positionality which has privileged one group (White men) and marginalized another group (women). Comparative analysis studies of feminist scholarship and its impact in various disciplines concluded that this dualism is well established (DuBois, 1983; Harding, 1986; Farnham, 1987; Glazer, 1991). Furthermore, other feminist scholars (Anderson & Collins, 2009; Harding, 1991; Turner, 2002) used gender as an organizing principle of hierarchy society.

In the case of Black women (most often found at the bottom of the hierarchy), they must be treated as a group unto themselves. As bell hooks (1981) noted, "In much of the literature written by White women on the 'woman question' from the 19th century to the present day, authors will refer to 'White men' but the word 'woman' when they really mean 'White woman.' Concurrently, the term 'Blacks' is often made synonymous with Black men" (p. 140). Furthermore, Collins (2000) noted that Black women as a group experience a world different from that of those who are not Black and female. She also found and experienced that Black women have long occupied marginal positions and argued that many Black female intellectuals have made use of their marginality, i.e., their "outsider within" status to produce Black feminist thought that reflects a special standpoint on self, family, and society.

Black Feminist Thought

Understanding the intersections of work and family in Black women's lives is key to clarifying the overarching economy of domination and leadership (Collins, 2000). In the early days of the women's movement, Black women were ignored and marginalized. Even in the 1913 Women's Suffrage March, the members of Delta Sigma Theta Sorority, Inc. were forced to march in the very back of the parade due to their skin color; while they were women, in the eyes of the dominant group, they were still Black women and needed to know their place. African American women have been addressing the concerns of White male and female domination and hegemony from the very beginning. There have been very few theoretical constructs or directions that have placed this segment of the population at the center of larger disciplines.

With a specific analysis of the discipline of leadership and leadership theories, Parker (2005) noted that there are issues with race-neutralizing theories as they relate to leadership in organizations. There are those studies that related to domination (taken-for-granted assumptions about superiority and inferiority), exclusion (of certain groups from the knowledge production process), and containment (practices that silence those who speak out against or in other ways resist oppression [Collins, 1998]). The popular feminist critiques of gender exclusive masculine leadership simply reinforce White middle-class feminine models that exclude the leadership of women who are not White. Thus, while the power of a feminist lens shows the ability to focus on the gaps and blank spaces of male-dominant culture, knowledge, and behavior (Gosetti & Rusch, 1995), centering the experience of the Black woman whose lived experience challenges Western ideals of femininity is important to disrupting the traditional notions of feminine and masculine leadership (Parker, 2005).

Intersectionality

Black women in leadership positions are an absolute necessity, yet unfortunately in many ways still an anomaly. As these women continue to take on these roles in leadership, there exists a multi-pronged identity with "competing agendas" (Tyson, 1998) that place race at the center while simultaneously considering gender as well as sexual orientation. These women are ever cognizant of the disparity they may face because of the color of their skin (Meyerson, 2001) their gender (Jones, 2003), and their sexual orientation (Alston, in press).

Gressgard (2008) noted that the feminist movement was criticized for its homogenizing and totalizing presupposition, and for silencing Black women in particular, by presuming an exclusionary (White, middle-class) concept of "woman." Thus, intersectionality, a term coined by Kimberle Crenshaw (1989), was developed based on Black women's political critique of feminism.

The paradigm of intersectionality (Collins, 1998; Crenshaw, 1991) helps to account for the complexity of the Black woman's lived experiences, recognizing that race, class, gender, and sexual orientation are markers of power creating intersecting lines or axes used to reinforce power relations and forms of oppression (Collins, 2000). Intersectionality, as noted by Collins, is a sociological theory suggesting that—and seeking to examine how —various socially and culturally constructed categories of discrimination interact on multiple and often simultaneous levels, contributing to systematic social inequality. Intersectionality holds that the classical models of oppression within society, such as those based on race, ethnicity, gender, religion, nationality, sexual orientation, class, or disability do not act independently of one another. Instead, these forms of oppression interrelate creating a system of oppression that reflects the "intersection" of multiple forms of discrimination. Furthermore, intersectionality "may shed light on the mutually constructing nature of systems of oppression, as well as social locations created by such mutual constructions" (Collins, 2000, p. 153). Black women in this context contribute to the knowledge base on leadership by referencing their experiences in these intersections and thus are situated as *knowers* (Collins, 2000). Thus, leadership theory becomes informed by these women's intersecting oppressions and their lived experiences.

Tempered Radicalism

Within this reality of intersectionality, Black women are often placed in environments of power differentials, and they use the power that is originally intended as a mechanism for oppression to be transformed into an effective vehicle for constructive change (Lorde, 1984). Meyerson and Scully (1995) identified this action as *tempered radicalism*, wherein there are "individuals who identify with and are committed to their organizations and also to a cause, community, or ideology that is fundamentally different from, and possibly at odds with the dominant culture of their organization" (p. 586); "they rock the boat and stay in the boat" (Meyerson, 2001, p. xi). These women are radical in their ideals but tempered in the fact that they work within the confines of their organizations (Jones, 2003). They have been tempered by time and experience, refined by the challenges, people, policies, and politics that they have faced. As Meyerson (2001) stated:

> Tempered radicals reflect important aspects of leadership that are absent in the more traditional portraits...it is more local, more diffuse, more opportunistic, and more humble than the activity attributed to the modern-day hero. This version of leadership depends...on qualities such as patience, self-knowledge, humility, flexibility, idealism, vigilance, and commitment...they are not lone heroes...and are quick to acknowledge that they cannot do it alone." (p. 171)

Tempered radicals are change agents who practice leadership in such ways that significant systemic change is far-reaching and long-lasting. These women rely on a strong core foundation with strong core values. They put their beliefs into action:

> The act of putting this part of themselves out in the world for affirmation and challenge often reminds them, and others, that they will not silence these valued parts of their selves and that they will not allow the dominant culture to define who they are. (Meyerson, 2001, p. 14)

This work actually brings about inspiration. So, African American female tempered radicals are not only change agents but also agents of inspiration. These women experience the "competing pulls" of being both effective, contributing organizational insiders and outsiders "because they represent ideals or agendas that are somehow at odds with the dominant culture" in their organizations (Meyerson, 2001, p. 5). They are quiet (not necessarily in voice, but in subtely of action) leaders that act as catalysts for new ideas, alternative perspectives, and organizational learning and change. Collins (1986) found that as "outsiders within," these women have a critical and creative edge that allows them to speak new "truths."

Yet, with the case of Black women, in particular, their absence and silence in leadership has been perpetuated by the contention that women (these women in particular) are trying to be leaders inside   hierarchical   organizations   that   promote   gender stratification by roles and maintains values and beliefs based on men's experiences; this incongruence creates social tension for women in leadership (Hart, 1995). Even more, these tempered radicals, according to Meyerson (2001), include women who refuse to act like men in male-dominated institutions and people of color who want to expand their boundaries of inclusion in predominantly White institutions. By analyzing gender as an invisible social construct in stratified roles, Hart argues that organizations apply deliberate and unconscious tactics to the socialization of new members–in this case Black women–that result in different types of responses. Three stages of responses are presented:

1. The encounter or anticipation state in which learning needs occur.
2. Adjustment or accommodation stage in which a new leader confronts "fitting in" to the established organizational culture.
3. The stabilization or role management level of social contracting of relationship with others in the organization.

In actuality, many Black women have rejected and continue to reject models of authority that are and have been based on unjust hierarchies. Black women activists such as Septima Clark, Ella Baker, Shirley Chisholm, and Angela Davis challenged the systems from within. As bell hooks (1989) aptly noted:

> We must be willing to critically examine anew the tensions that arise when we simultaneously try to educate in such a way as to ensure the progression of a liberatory feminist movement and work to create a respected place for feminist scholarship within academic institutions. We must also examine the tensions that arise when we try to subvert while working to keep jobs, to be promoted, etc. These practical concerns are factors that influence and/or determine the type of scholarship deemed important. Often attempts to mediate or reconcile these tensions leads to frustration, despair, cooperation, complicity, or shifts in allegiance. (p. 40)

This Context and This Truth

Thus it is within this context of social justice, feminism, Black feminist thought, and tempered radicalism where two prophets, Audre Lorde and Barbara Jordan, rise to speak truth to power and to make known their rightful place in the discourse and praxis of leadership. It is within their "herstories" that the truth comes to light on how we should really view leadership in this particular lens.

Herstory–Audre Lorde:
"Warrior Radical Fighting for Justice"

> Those of us who stand outside the circle of this society's definition of acceptable women; those of us who have been forged in the crucibles of difference—those of us who are poor, who are lesbians, who are Black, who are older—know that survival is not an academic skill...For the master's tools will not dismantle the master's house. They will never allow us to bring about genuine change. Lorde (1984, 2007)

No truer words have ever been spoken than these from the prophetic voice of Audre Lorde–self-described as a Black, lesbian, mother, warrior, and poet. In an African naming ceremony before her death, she took the name *Gamba Adisa*, meaning "warrior: she who makes her meaning known." In her identity as "warrior," she made her meaning known via her battles against racism, sexism, heterosexism, ageism, classism, i.e., oppression in its many forms, as well as against her cancer. Lorde (1983) famously noted that there is no hierarchy of oppression. She stated:

> I was born Black, and a woman. I am trying to become the strongest person I can become to live the life I have been given and to help effect change toward a livable future for this earth and for my children. As a Black, lesbian, feminist, socialist, poet, mother of two including one boy and a member of an interracial couple, I usually find myself part of some group in which the majority defines me as deviant, difficult, inferior or just plain "wrong."

From my membership in all of these groups I have learned that oppression and the intolerance of difference come in all shapes and sexes and colors and sexualities; and that among those of us who share the goals of liberation and a workable future for our children, there can be no hierarchies of oppression. I have learned that sexism (a belief in the inherent superiority of one sex over all others and thereby its right to dominance) and heterosexism (a belief in the inherent superiority of one pattern of loving over all others and thereby its right to dominance) both arise from the same source as racism—a belief in the inherent superiority of one race over all others and thereby its right to dominance. (Lorde, as cited in Byrd, Cole, & Guy-Sheftall, 2009, p. 219)

Issues of oppression continue to dominate our society. We as women still earn less than our male counterparts, issues still abound around "race" and skin color, interracial marriage is still problematic (though legal), LGBTQ oppression still reigns, the divide between the *haves* and *have nots* is growing daily while the middle class shrinks. Social justice seems oxymoronic and elusive.

An Outsider with an Inside View

Born on February 18, 1934 to Caribbean immigrants, Audre Geraldine Lorde, the youngest of three daughters, came into this traditional world organization (the family organization, the cultural organization, the societal organization) as a committed radical change agent. She was in the world but not of the world; she was born as a tempered radical and to become leader for social justice. She was, as Meyerson (2001) describes, an "organizational insider" who is treated as an outsider (Lorde as *Sister Outsider*) because her values are "at odds with the dominant culture" (p. 5). At an early age, Lorde questioned religious ideas, argued and reasoned with the Sisters of the Blessed Sacrament at St. Mark's Academy Elementary School, an all-Black school except for the Whites who ran the school (DeVeaux, 2004). Furthermore, tempered radicals feel misaligned with the dominant culture due to issues surrounding their identities, i.e., race, gender, sexual orientation, class, age, etc. Lorde often found herself outside the contested realm of social relations, yet she embraced her status and positioned herself in a space to effect change on the ways in which we now talk about, write about, and think about issues of social justice and oppression.

In the midst of the overwhelmingly White feminist movement, Lorde spoke out as a Black, lesbian feminist whose views were not congruent with the power structure that was in place. She was concerned with the "specificity of the lived experience of Black women" (Byrd, 2009, p. 10). Dealing with the issues of racism and sexism in the feminist movement, Lorde (1984/2007) clearly stated, "Black feminism is not white feminism in Blackface. Black women have particular and legitimate issues which affect our lives as Black women..." (p. 60). Furthermore, she continued, "When I say I am a Black feminist, I mean I recognize that my power as well as my primary oppressions come as a result of my Blackness as well as my womanness, and therefore my struggles on both these fronts are inseparable" (as cited in Andrews, Smith Foster, & Harris, 2001, p. 262). She recognized the dismissal of the Black woman's perspective in feminism in particular when she responded to Daly's (1978) *Gyn/Ecology: The Metaethics of Radical Feminism* in noting that

> The history of white women who are unable to hear Black women's words, or to maintain dialogue with us, is long and discouraging...the assumption that the herstory and myth of all women to call upon for power and background, and that nonwhite women and our herstories are noteworthy only as decorations, or examples of female victimization....When patriarchy dismisses us, it encourages our murderers. When radical lesbian feminist theory dismisses us, it encourages its own demise. This dismissal stands as a real block to communication between us. (Lorde, 1984/2007, pp. 66-69)

She clearly recognized and experienced that the lives of Black women were different from their White counterparts and that it was in no way a parallel. The marginalized lives of the "other" could not be counted in the normative view of *womanness* which was White and middle class.

Talking Back and Talking "Out"

The act of "talking back" is considered being sassy in many African American families and talking back to one's elder can land you in serious trouble, as you are perceived to believe that you are "grown" before your time. However, Walker (1984) defined this as womanist behavior, which is to be independent, responsible, in charge, and to act grown up. In coming to voice and being able to "talk back and talk out," bell hooks (1990) pointed out that there are three interrelated components–breaking silence about oppression, developing self-reflexive speech, and confronting or "talking back" to elite discourses. Finding this place of voice Patricia Hill Collins (1998) noted that belonging yet not belonging presents peculiar challenges. This indeed does describe the life of Audre Lorde, yet she used her voice to traverse the seas of oppression and meet challenges head on. In her paper "The Transformation of Silence into Language and Action," Lorde (1980) shortly after her diagnosis of breast cancer wrote,

> I have come to believe over and over again that what is most important to me must be spoken, made verbal and shared, even at the risk of having it bruised or misunderstood. That the speaking profits me, beyond any other effect. I am standing here as a Black lesbian poet and the meaning of all that waits upon the fact that I am still alive, and might not have been. (as cited in Byrd, Cole, & Guy-Sheftall, 2009, p. 39)

Her journey to being an out lesbian was fraught with ups and downs as life goes for anyone trying to not only figure who they are but also accept who they are. Though she had known for the majority of her life, she finally publicly came out as a lesbian at a poetry reading in 1973 in New York (De Veaux, 2004). Thus, by situating herself in the knowing and understanding of who she was and what she brought to the world, Lorde was trailblazer for those of us who are Black and have multiple axes of identities to follow in her footsteps and to stand on her shoulders. The epistemological underpinnings, the ways in which we come to know, and the influence of what is known becomes a critical unit of analysis as we explore the social and political transformation of leadership. It is within this "positionality" where an analysis of Lorde's multilayered "outness" informs praxis.

Positionality theory contributes an effective framework for gaining insight into the multiple perspectives of leadership, culture and schooling. This concept, built upon "standpoint theory" (an observation from one position) expands the lens to include the multi-faceted, overlapping identities, as "intersectionality" (Crenshaw, 1989). Positionality theory, infers that power relationships are fluid and dynamic, affected by historical and social changes, resist dichotomies (repression vs. oppression), are transactional (negotiated and socially constructed), and can be transformed. Kezar (2000) used positionality theory as a framework for studying and defining leadership. "Positioned individuals...possessing multifaceted identities...within a particular context...influenced by conditions of power...construct leadership in unique...and collective ways simultaneously" (p. 727).

The position of leadership as a genre and concept has been studied in view of the macroculture pushing and leaving the "other" microcultures at the margins rather than recognizing their shared contexts and histories and power relationships. Given this problem, how can we address the research that supports effective and efficacious leadership by women of color for example whose identities, being Black and female, inform in culturally specific ways their leadership beliefs and actions? To address this, it is imperative to frame the discussion by "talking back," highlighting, for example, the ways that race, gender, and sexual orientation as cogent units of analysis in positionality theory, intersecting with leadership theory and societal cultural influences must be at the center of transformative models for the teaching, research, and reform of the field of leadership.

As a knowingly positioned individual, Lorde brought to the fore a focus on issues of race, gender, and sexual orientation. In a time that it was not "fashionable" or "accepted," she was very clear to identify exactly who she was: an out and proud Black lesbian feminist. She was intentional in her use of language to make visible the invisible. Byrd (2009) noted that her political objective was to reduce the isolation and fear that most often defines the lives of those who were also Black lesbian feminists. She said that she wanted others to know that they were not alone (Lorde, 1988).

As a warrior radical and leader for social justice, Lorde headed off and addressed oppression and discrimination. In "Scratching the Surface: Some Notes on Barriers to Women and Loving," (Lorde, 2007) defined racism, sexism, heterosexism, and homophobia:

- Racism–the belief in the inherent superiority of one race over all others and thereby the right to dominance;
- Sexism–the belief in the inherent superiority of one sex and thereby the right to dominance;
- Heterosexism–a belief in the inherent superiority of one form of loving over all others and thereby the right to dominance;
- Homophobia–a terror surrounding feelings of love for members of the same sex and thereby hatred of those feelings in others. (p. 45)

Early experiences with racism shaped her thinking and her actions. She was the first Black student at St. Catherine's Catholic school in 1945 and the experiences there would "shape her later ideas about women, community, and difference" (DeVeaux, 2004, p. 23). At the all-white school, she dealt with racial incidents receiving secret notes telling her that she smelled. Upon going to the authorities, the nuns, she was told that Black people did smell differently than Whites, but it was cruel to point out something to her that she could not help.

Other experiences in life also shaped her outlook on race and racism. In 1968 she was granted "poet-in-residence" status at Tougaloo College, a historically Black college in Jackson, Mississippi where the Freedom Riders had been six years prior. She was afraid of the south and rightfully so. She was married to a white man and they had produced two interracial children. Though they were not with her, she felt that in order to be an "authentic" leader that she needed to share that information with her students. It was a time of unrest and the Black students were embracing a more militant stance. Yet, they *all* had to deal with the gunshots at night outside the college from the members of the White Citizens' Council. But, out of this time at Tougaloo grew what would become Audre Lorde's theory of difference (DeVeaux, 2004).

On a trip to Ghana with Frances Clayton (her white female partner) and her children Lorde experienced racism as well. Lorde was often presumed to be Clayton's servant. When being served at restaurants, the waiters and/or hotel personnel would serve Frances first, look to her to make decisions, as well as to pay the bill while simultaneously ignoring Lorde (DeVeaux, 2004). This deeply offended Lorde; yet, it was still on the continent of Africa, the Motherland, that she was able to find her spiritual connection.

Unafraid, Lorde named the demons and called them out. She named the various stereotypes that have been attributed to Black lesbians, and in this naming she also identified the origin: "The terror of Black lesbians is buried in that deep inner place where we have been taught to fear all indifference—to kill or ignore it" (Lorde, 1988, p. 21; Byrd, 2009). In a speech during the 1979 first National March on Washington for Lesbian and Gay Rights, Lorde brought together the ideologies of civil rights, feminist, and lesbian and gay liberation movements. Again in the 1983 March on Washington, which marked the 20th anniversary of the 1963 march, Lorde spoke for the National Coalition of Black Lesbians and Gay Men where she noted that the current event openly joined the Black civil rights movement and the gay civil rights movement. As bell hooks (1989) noted, one must "talk back" about the suffering that we experience. Lorde (1978) spoke up and out being clear that "when we are silent, we are still afraid, so it is better to speak remembering we were never meant to survive" (p. 32). For her "words had an energy and power and she [I] came to respect that power early. Pronouns, nouns, and verbs were citizens of different countries, who really got together to make a new world" (Hammond, 1981). In the essay, "My Words Will Be There," Lorde summed it up:

I write for myself. I write for myself and my children and for as many people as who can read me. When I say myself, I mean not only the Audre who inhabits my body but all those *feisty, incorrigible, beautiful Black women* who insist on standing up and saying I am and you can't wipe me out, no matter how irritating I am.

I feel a responsibility for myself, for those people who can now read and feel and need what I have to say, and for women and men who come after me. But primarily I think of my responsibility in terms of women because there are many voices for men. There are few voices for women and particularly few voices for Black women, speaking from the center of consciousness, for *I am* out to the *we are*. (as cited in Byrd, Cole, & Guy Sheftall, 2009, p. 168)

Still in her role as a tempered radical, Lorde denounced both the homophobia in the civil rights movement as well as the racism in the gay and lesbian movement. Because of the intersectionality of her identities and her "out" stance to being an authentic person and living authentically, there was no way that she not be any of who she was–*Black and female and lesbian and feminist and mother and daughter of immigrants and educator and cancer survivor and activist*–so she had to fight within that context. She stated, "...I am not one piece of myself. I cannot be simply a Black person and not be a woman too, nor can I be a woman without being a lesbian" (Byrd, et al., 2009, p. 162). Furthermore she keenly observed:

Yet the time is long past when any of us can afford the luxury of exclusive oppression....We can not love "our people" unless we love each of us ourselves, unless I love each piece of myself, those I wish to keep and those I wish to change–for the survival is the ability to encompass difference, to encompass change without destruction. (Lorde, as cited in Byrd, 2009, pp. 23-26).

Lorde understood what "talking back and out" meant for those who inhabited or were forced into liminal spaces. In "A Litany for Survival," she stated: "When we speak we are afraid our words will not be heard nor welcomed but when we are silent we are still afraid. So it is better to speak remembering we were never meant to survive" (Lorde, 1978, p. 32).

Speak she did and does as we continue to listen.

Herstory–Barbara Jordan: The Voice of Justice and the Conscience of a Nation

My single greatest accomplishment is, I mean this quite sincerely...it is representing hundreds, thousands, of heretofore nameless, faceless, voiceless people...The letters I enjoy most are those who write and say, "For the first time, I feel there is somebody talking for me." If I've done anything, I have tried to represent them. – Barbara Jordan

Ethics and social justice intersected and guided the life of Barbara Charline Jordan. She lived by a simple creed: "Ethical behavior means being honest, telling the truth, and doing what you said you were going to do." The word ethics is derived from the Greek word *ethos* meaning customs, conduct, or character. Ethics are simply a set of moral principles that guide our decisions regarding right and wrong. Northouse (2007) noted that with regard to leadership, ethics has to do with what leaders do and who leaders are, the nature of leaders' behavior and their virtuousness. Beck and Murphy (1997) viewed ethical leadership as a two-step process. First, leaders must view ethics as a set of fundamental principles that guide their decision making process. Second, they contend that leaders must embrace ethics as a necessary element of character. In fact, they state, "Ethics is less about making decisions using objective principles and more about living morally in specific situations" (p. 33). Throughout her public and political life, Barbara Jordan instilled in Americans everywhere the hope for ethical leadership and racial equality and harmony. As Holmes (2000) noted, Jordan approached ethics as moral instincts functioning as moral discernments which initiated informed and morally relevant choices. Furthermore, Jordan understood the rules that governed the social order; she identified the values that would enhance community life; and she chose means that were congruent with the ends sought (as cited in Anderson, n.d.).

According to Ngunjiri (2010), it has been noted by researchers that Black women leaders, particularly those who have been invested in social justice agendas, tended to be tempered radicals as they acted as change agents from within structures that were inhospitable to them as women and as racial minorities. As a tempered radical, Jordan stayed true to who she was and who she was raised to be. She did as Meyerson (2001) identified—resisted quietly, not in voice, but manner (actively, audibly, and forcefully), and remained true to her authentic self. Meyerson stated that "quiet forms of resistance can and do often contribute to learning and adaptation" (p. 38). Jordan's form of psychological resistance led her to be successful as the first Black woman elected to the Texas Senate in 1966. When speaking with a reporter who questioned her about how she dealt with colleagues who were both racist and sexist, she replied, "I have a tremendous amount of faith in my own capacity. I know how to read and write and think, so I have no fear" (as cited in Gates & West, 2000, p. 300). Jordan also resisted via her leadership behavior. Her style was to lead by example with her ethics and morals guiding her steps.

Her steps were ordered by her upbringing. Barbara Jordan was the youngest of three daughters born to Benjamin and Arlyne Jordan in Houston's Fifth Ward within a very tight knit family and community. Her early years were tied to family, church, education, and hard work. Her work ethic and her desire for justice were developed and nurtured through the time and experiences that she shared with her maternal grandfather, John Ed Patten. She proudly noted, "...I am the composite of my experience and all the people who had something to do with it...." Grandpa Patten had more than a little to do with it, as theirs was an attachment from the very beginning of her birth on February 21, 1936. Unlike her father and other grandfather, this maternal grandfather was not a part of the churchgoing core, yet he was a strong believer in the teachings of Jesus the Christ. So as her sisters who on Sunday afternoons learned their Bible verses and books of the Bible at church, Barbara learned life lessons from Grandpa Patten who would say: "You don't have to do that" (Jordan & Hearon, 1979, p. 4), as she spent her Sunday afternoons with him working on his mule cart collecting junk from the various Houston neighborhoods. Her business acumen, self-reliance, and independence were honed via the time that she spent with him. A guiding principle for her life and lasting legacy that he gave her was "You just trot your own horse and don't get into the same rut as everyone else" (p. 7). With regards to marriage, he further underscored this guiding principle with, "Do not take a boss. Do not marry. Look at your mother" (Rogers, 2000, p. 91). Thus, the refining of her tempered radicalism was in effect from an early age, she did indeed "trot" to her own horse throughout her life as she emphatically stated, "I never intended to become a run-of-the-mill person."

The Voice: An Ethic of Responsibility

> We must exchange the philosophy of excuse—what I am is beyond my control for the philosophy of responsibility. –Barbara Jordan

According to Max Weber, an ethic of responsibility "acknowledges value obligations, but assumes the absence of any given hierarchy of values and the inevitability of value conflict as the context for moral endeavor" (Starr, 1999, p. 407). This ethic of responsibility requires that if one is placed in a position of power, then one has the responsibility to do the work, which aligns with Weber's notion of social action as overt action as well as the failure to act and passively acquiesce (Alston, in press). Jordan in a 1996 commencement address for Texas Tech University's Law School articulated her definition of an ethic of responsibility. She stated:

> Service to others is a recognition of the dignity of the individual. Everything that we do—our actions have consequences. And those consequences affect other people. There is an interconnectedness between each one of us which can not be abolished. No matter what you wish or what you desire we are connected. Since what you do affects me regardless of your intent, I would prefer then that you act with a responsibility that forecloses a bad outcome. Responsibility is a universal value. It is a universal virtue and no one can escape it. It applies to everyone. But it is especially crucial to those of us who live in this Democracy because of its high reliance on the individual.

Thus, within the context of this ethic of responsibility, using the power of her voice and her ability to take oratory to another level, Barbara Jordan broke barriers of race and gender. The *New*

York Times (Clines, 1996) described her oratory as "Churchillian." Another writer (Grady, 1996) suggested that her deep, booming voice could galvanize listeners "as though Winston Churchill had been reincarnated as a Black woman from Texas." The power of her voice and the strength of her words coupled with her ethical and social beliefs have left a lasting and eternal legacy. As Senator Barbara Boxer (1996) stated on Jordan's passing:

> Barbara Jordan was a voice for common ground, for the ties that bind. Hers were powerful, healing, uplifting words that challenged and inspired women and minorities, indeed all Americans, to reach for something higher and to believe in themselves and their own ability to change the world and make it a better place.

Patricia Hill Collins (1998) in relating Black women, power, and voice, asked one question: "What are the implications of 'coming to voice' as a trope for Black women's praxis?" While Barbara Jordan did not commit to a particular epistemological stance or identify as a feminist, Black feminist, or womanist, her words and actions speak to these areas. For African American women, the development and use of voice has related to her strategies for survival, resistance, and change since slavery (Parker, 2005). Voice for Black women is used as tempered radical and resistance strategy. Because of the oppressions that Black women have dealt with their existence from the beginning of time, an oratorical and oral tradition has been their weapon of choice and survival. This Black feminist orality (Fulton, 2006) has been a form of empowerment to speak truth to power and express self and experience all ultimately in the larger milieu of an ethic of responsibility.

In Collins's (1998) view "coming to voice" is the idea of "breaking silence" usually in the context of an individual speaking out against some kind of institutional knowledge, with a view to advancing the cause of a collective group. An example of this would be to "experience speaking out against authority." Thus speaking out in this sense is not a discovery of inequality which is then verbalized, but rather a public testimonial (i.e., Jordan's Watergate speech and keynote addresses at the Democratic

Conventions) about unequal power relations which have long been understood by marginalized groups. Breaking silence is a part of the lived experience for African American female tempered radicals. Audre Lorde (1984, 2007) also made note of the breaking of silence and difference stating:

> The fact that we are here and I speak these words is an attempt to break that silence and bridge some of those difference between us, for it makes no difference which immobilizes us, but silence. And there are so many silences to be broken. (p. 40)

For Lorde, silence was the enemy to progressive mobilization and thus the mute response to difference. In alignment with this, Jordan (1976) positioned herself by standing in the gap and speaking for those who could not protect themselves as it was her responsibility to do so:

> Many fear the future. Many are distrustful of their leaders and believe that their voices are never heard. Many seek only to satisfy their private wants, to satisfy their private interests. But this is the great danger America faces–that we will cease to be one nation and become instead a collection of interest groups, each seeking to satisfy private wants. If that happens, who then will speak for America? Who then will speak for the common good?

Like other tempered radicals, Jordan made the difficult choices about when and how to "speak 'truths' and raise issues that have been suppressed" and when and how to remain silent without falling into a systemic collusion with their own cooptation and subordination (Meyerson, 2001, p. 76). This was most evident in her now infamous Watergate speech (1974) "Opening Statement to the House Judiciary Committee Proceedings on the Impeachment of Richard Nixon." Holmes (2000) noted that in this speech:

> Jordan situates herself as a protagonist who symbolically stands for national ideals in opposition to rampant abuses of political power. The speech positions her as an emblematic figure, the outsider heroine who speaks the unspeakable and acts as a focal point for public opinion and moral discourse. (p. 47)

Barbara Jordan's legacy is the example of her life of public service working toward the greater good within a higher ethical call and responsibility; a call for "principled pluralism." She challenged herself and others to live up to a potentially transformative concept of public life (Holmes, 2000).

The Life: An Ethic of Care and Justice

> As we have listened for centuries to the voices of men and the theories of development that their experience informs, so we have come more recently to notice not only the silence of women but the different voice of women lies in the truth of an ethic of care, the tie between relationship and responsibility, and the origins of aggression in the failure of connection. The failure to see the different reality of women's lives and to hear the differences in their voices stems in part from the assumption that there is a single mode of social experience and interpretation...While an ethic of just process from the premise of equality–that everyone should be treated the same–an ethic of care rests on the premise of nonviolence that no one should be hurt. (Gilligan, 1993, pp. 173-174)

Barbara Jordan lived a life committed to an ethic of care and an ethic of justice. An ethic of care is a normative ethical theory; that is, a theory about what makes actions right or wrong, yet emphasizes the importance of relationships, which aligns with Jordan's innate sense of right and wrong and of "oughtness" (Sherman, 2007, p. 8). This ethic of care is central to Black women's lives as it "suggests that personal expressiveness, emotions and empathy are central to the knowledge validation process" (Collins, 1990, p. 215). According to Gilligan (1982), a care orientation reflects the presence of benevolence and compassion. An ethic of care recognizes and responds to a need. Jordan took this charge to heart and to action.

Kohlberg (1984) noted that a justice orientation concerned fairness and impartiality. It deals with moral choices through a measure of rights of the people involved and chooses the solution that seems to damage the least number of people. In this case, justice means liberating others from injustice and orienting oneself away from biases and partial passions and toward universal ethical principles (Siddle Walker & Snarey, 2004).

Justice was a daily practice for Barbara Jordan as it was her vocation and avocation. For Jordan justice and care went hand-in-hand. In defining justice, she called it fairness and the first virtue of all human institutions. Furthermore justice requires caring, social responsibility, all in joint action. In marrying her care and her justice orientations, Jordan worked for several causes and met oppression head on. She proposed and helped pass legislation dealing with social change. She helped reform public assistance programs and protect workers' wages. She also opposed legislation that would have made it harder for Blacks and Latin Americans to vote. At the 1992 Democratic Convention, in her speech "Change: from What to What," she called for national unity:

> We are one, we Americans, we're one, and we reject any intruder who seeks to divide us on the basis of race and color. We honor cultural identity–we always have, we always will. But, separatism is not allowed –separatism is not the American way. We must not allow ideas like political correctness to divide us and cause us to reverse hard-won achievements in human rights and civil rights.

Within her justice orientation, in addition to working to pass key amendments to the Voting Rights Act, she also played a significant role in establishing mandatory Civil Rights Act enforcement procedures for the Law Enforcement Assistance Administration and the Office of Revenue Sharing.

Jordan refereed to justice as the "flagship principle" and the "the highest ideal for society" (Sherman, 2007, p. 66). Justice for Jordan was a part of the oxygen that she breathed; it was her sustainer. It was the vocation, a divine calling, that she had chosen and the life that she lived. She noted in "Justice," a speech given to the National Association of Attorneys General Convention in 1976, that:

> Justice is one of the first words in our Constitution, one of the first principles upon which this nation was founded. It is something that we have been working very hard to achieve for the last two centuries, yet, today, we are uncertain about what it is and how to achieve it.

Over time she had the opportunity to reconsider her stances on justice in our system. In 1976 her notion of justice concerned the nuts and bolts of a functioning system. However, by 1996 in "The Obligations of Inter-Generational Justice," she identified justice as a virtue that is synonymous with fairness (Holmes, 2000). According to Jordan, "each citizen gets justice and justice is denied no one" is what our system of government seeks to guarantee (Jordan, as cited in Holmes, 2000, p. 102). Given this evolved perspective, she noted that justice could not stand alone as a practical value, it must have the component of caring. This evolution also began to include an ethic of love: to be steadfast, committed, accountable and active. Fletcher (1966) found love to be the supreme ethic among many ethical demands. Furthermore, Cornett and Thomas (1995) noted that as a basis for ethics, love–along with dignity, justice, and equality/freedom–are core values that transcend cultures and are manifest in leadership.

This triumvirate–the ethics of care, justice, and love–made manifest in Barbara Jordan's practice was evident in her fight for a reauthorization to the 1965 Voting Rights Act and for Immigration Reform. She fought for and won inclusion of minority languages in the Voting Rights Act. This reauthorization's addition now required voting ballots to include minority languages where at least 5% of the population did not speak English as their first language. She also supported the Community Reinvestment Act of 1977, legislation that required banks to lend and make services available to underserved poor and minority communities. This desire to stop racial injustice as well as other oppression of marginalized groups was rooted in her own lived experience. As one was finally included in "We the People" (Jordan, 1974), her experiences growing up in the segregated Fifth Ward of Houston and even having graduated from Boston University with a law degree and not being offered positions by White law firms in Houston became the foundation and springboard for her activism. Holmes (2000) noted that Barbara Jordan did not take on the persona of a victim, but she used these experiences to generate "positive and self-sustaining responses to oppression" (p. 5).

In 1993, President Clinton appointed Jordan to chair the U.S. Commission on Immigration Reform (CIR). She chaired the commission into 1995, shortly before her death, and she would never see the final report. In her commitment to neighbor and country, love was the foundation. For her "E Pluribus Unum" was a living phrase. We must love (be committed, steadfast, accountable, and active) our fellow man because it is our charge as humans and "the rent we pay for living." Her fight for immigration reform was rooted in her belief for the common good. She felt that the U.S. should end both the chain migration and the Diversity Visa Lottery program. Additionally they should enforce strict deportation policies not just for illegal aliens convicted of aggravated felonies and other crimes, but for all border/visa violators. She also opposed welfare programs for illegal aliens, as well as concrete employer sanctions. She stated: "We believe legal immigration is in the national interest, but see illegal immigration as a threat both to our long tradition of immigration and to our commitment to the rule of law" (Jordan, 1995, as cited in Sherman, 2007, p. 60). While some did not agree with her (or the Commission's) stance on immigration, particularly some in the Latino community, there was no denying her legacy as one Hispanic leader noted when Jordan passed away: "This (her stance on immigration) doesn't take away from her greatness in our community" (as cited in Sherman, 2007, p. 56). She never hesitated to use her voice to say what she meant or what she felt whether or not people agreed with her.

A Spectacle of Greatness

Generally speaking, the idea of "making a spectacle of oneself" has a negative connotation. Not so in the life of Barbara Charline Jordan. Max Sherman (2007) in *Barbara Jordan: Speaking the Truth with Eloquent Thunder* referred to his friend and colleague as a "Spectacle of Greatness." He noted:

> By holding up Barbara Jordan as a "spectacle of greatness," those of us who call ourselves "public servants" take on the mantle of telling the truth, whether we be president, special counsel, judge, elected or

appointed official, public employee; we are honest; we tell the truth; we protect and care for the public...If we call ourselves "public servants," we should live our lives in such a way that whenever we retire...we are remembered for living and conducting our public business in the most honorable, ethical way. (p. 9)

She made a "spectacle of herself" and the world is better for her having done so. The voice is not silent. It still speaks in the 21st century. Bill Moyers' remarks at Jordan's 1996 memorial said it best:

...The body dies: "dust to dust and ashes to ashes." But the voice that speaks for justice joins the music of the spheres. What does the universe even know of justice unless informed by a Barbara Jordan?...On matters of meaning and morality, the universe is dumbstruck, the planets silent. Our notions of right and wrong, of how to live together, come from our prophets, not from the planets. It is the human voice that commands justice to roll down "like waters, and righteousness like a mighty stream." And what a voice this was! (as cited in Sherman, 2007, pp. 89-90)

Points to Consider

1. How do you define social justice? Is it an inclusive or exclusive definition?
2. Relate the concept of tempered radicalism to your position as a leader in your organization.
3. Give examples of current leaders who practice and promote social justice.
4. What is your professional code of ethics? Your personal code of ethics? If you do not have one, then write one and share.
5. What is the state of ethics and leadership in the 21st century?
6. View/discuss the Jordan speech for the 1974 Impeachment hearing for President Nixon. What are the relevant lessons for leadership today?
7. Discuss and unpack Lorde's notion of "no hierarchy of oppression."

Suggested Readings

Alston, J. A. (in press). An ethic of responsibility: A Black lesbian scholar ponders the intersection of racism and heterosexism in educational leadership. In R. Johnson & S. Jackson (Eds.). *The Black professoriat: Negotiating a habitable space.* New York: Peter Lang.

Boxer, B. (1996, January 22). Life of Barbara Jordan. *Congressional Record Online.* Retrieved from http://www.elf.net/bjordan/boxer.html

Brown, M. E., Treviño, L. K., & Harrison, D. A. (2005). Ethical leadership: A social learning perspective for construct development and testing. *Organizational Behavior and Human Decision Processes, 97*(2), 117-134.

Byrd, R. P. (2009). Create your own fire: Audre Lorde and the tradition of Black radical thought. In R. Byrd, J. B. Cole, & B. Guy-Sheftall (Eds.). *I am your sister: Collected and unpublished writings of Audre Lorde* (pp.3-36). New York: Oxford University Press.

Byrd, R., Cole, J. B., &. Guy-Sheftall, B. (Eds.). (2009). *I am your sister: Collected and unpublished writings of Audre Lorde.* New York: Oxford University Press.

Canas, K. A. (2002). *Barbara Jordan, Shirley Chisholm, and Lani Guinier: Crafting identification through the rhetorical interbraiding of value.* Ph.D. dissertation, The University of Utah.

Card, C. (1988). Women's voices and ethical ideals: Must we mean what we say? *Ethics, 99,* 125.

Chow, R. P. K. (2003). *The personal is political is ethical: Experiential revaluation and embodied witnessing in illness narratives.* M.A. dissertation, Simon Fraser University (Canada).

Clines, F. X. (1996, January 18). Barbara Jordan Dies at 59; Her Voice Stirred the Nation. *New York Times.* Retrieved from http://www.nytimes.com

Collins, P. H. (1986). Learning from the outsider within. *Journal of Social Problems, 33*(6), S14-S32.

Collins, P. H. (1998). *Fighting words: Black women and the search for justice.* Minneapolis: University of Minnesota Press.

Collins, P. H. (2000). *Black feminist thought: Knowledge, consciousness and the politics of empowerment* (2nd ed.). New York: Routledge.

Crenshaw, K. (1989). Demarginalizing the intersection of race and sex: A Black feminist critique of antidiscrimination doctrine, feminist theory, and antiracist politics. *University of Chicago Legal Forum.*

Dantley, M. E., & Tillman, L. C. (2006). Social justice and moral transformative leadership. In C. Marshall and M. Oliva (Eds.), *Leadership for social justice: Making revolutions in education.* Boston: Pearson.

Denhardt, K. (1988). *The ethics of the public service: Resolving moral dilemmas in public organizations.* New York: Greenwood.

DeVeaux, A. (2004). *Warrior poet: A biography of Audre Lorde.* New York: W. W. Norton.

Du Bois, B. (1983). Passionate scholarship: Notes on values, knowing and method in feminist social science. In G. Bowles & R. D. Klein (Eds.), *Theories of women's studies* (pp. 105-116). London: Routledge.

Flanagan, O., & Jackson, K. (1987). Justice, care, and gender: The Kohlberg-Gilligan debate revisited. *Ethics, 97,* 622.

Fraser, E., Hornsby, J., & Lovibond, S. (Eds.). (1992). *Ethics: A feminist reader.* Cambridge, MA: Blackwell.

Fulton, D. S. (2006). *Speaking power: Black feminist orality in women's narratives of slavery.* New York: SUNY.

Gates, H. L., & West, C. (2000). *The African American century: How Black Americans have shaped our country.* New York: Simon & Shuster.

Giddings, P. (1996). *When and where I enter: The impact of Black women on race and sex in America.* New York: Harper Paperbacks.

Gilligan, C. (1982). *In a different voice.* Cambridge, MA: Harvard University Press.

Gilligan, C. (1993). *In a different voice.* (2nd Edition). Cambridge, MA: Harvard University Press.

Gumbs, A. (2010). *We can learn to mother ourselves: The queer survival of Black feminism 1968-1996*. Ph.D. dissertation, Duke University, United States-North Carolina. Retrieved December 20, 2010, from Dissertations & Theses: A&I. (Publication No. AAT 3398433).

Hammond, K. (1981). Audre Lorde: Interview. *Denver Quarterly, 16*, 10-27.

Harding, S. (1991). *Whose science? Whose knowledge? Thinking from women's lives*. Ithaca, NY: Cornell University Press.

Harmon, M. (1995). *Responsibility as paradox*. Thousand Oaks, CA: Sage.

Holmes, B. A. (1998). *Barbara Jordan's speeches, 1974-1995: Ethics, public religion and jurisprudence*. Ph.D. dissertation, Vanderbilt University.

Holmes, B. A. (2000). *A private woman in public spaces: Barbara Jordan's speeches on ethics, public religion, and law*. Harrisburg, PA: Trinity Press International.

Horwitz, L. D. (1998). *Transforming appearance into rhetorical argument: Rhetorical criticism of public speeches of Barbara Jordan, Lucy Parsons, and Angela Y. Davis*. Ph.D. dissertation, Northwestern University, United States–Illinois. Retrieved December 20, 2010, from Dissertations & Theses: A&I. (Publication No. AAT 9913812).

Hune, S. (1997). Higher education as gendered space: Asian American women and everyday inequities. In C. R. Ronai, B. A. Zsembik, & J. R. Feagin (Eds.), *Everyday sexism in the third millennium* (pp. 181-196). New York: Routledge.

Jones, C., & Shorter-Gooden, K. (2004). *Shifting: The double lives of Black women in America*. New York: Harper Perennial.

Jordan, B. (1976, July 12). Democratic Convention Keynote Address: "Who will speak for the common good?" New York.

Jordan, B. (1992, July 13). Democratic Convention Keynote Address: "Change: From what to what?" New York.

Jordan, B. (1996). Ethic of responsibility. 27 *Tex. Tec L. Rev.* 1435

Jordan, B., & Hearon, S. (1979). *Barbara Jordan: A self-portrait*. New York: Doubleday.

Jos, P. H., & Hines, S. M., Jr. (1993). Care, justice, and public administration. *Administration & Society, 25*(3), 373-392.

Lorde, A. (1978). *The Black unicorn: Poems.* New York: W. W. Norton.

Lorde, A. (1980). *The cancer journals.* San Francisco, CA: Spinsters Ink.

Lorde, A. (1983). There is no hierarchy of oppression. In *From homophobia and education.* New York: Council on Interracial Books for Children.

Lorde, A. (1984). *Sister outsider.* Trumansburg, NY: Crossing Press.

Lorde, A. (1988). *A burst of light.* Ithaca, NY: Firebrand.

Lorde, A. (1988). Scratching the surface: Some notes on barriers to women and loving. In *Sister outsider* (pp. 45-52). Berkeley, CA: Crossing Press.

Lorde, A. (2007). *Sister outsider.* Berkeley, CA: Crossing Press.

Marshall, C. & Ward, M. (2004). "Yes, but....": Education leaders discuss social justice. *Journal of School Leadership, 14 (3), 530-563.*

Meyerson, D. E. (2001). *Tempered radicals: How people use difference to inspire change at work.* Boston: Harvard Business School Press.

Ngunjiri, F. W. (2010). *Women's spiritual leadership in Africa: Tempered radicals and critical servant leaders.* New York: SUNY Press.

Noddings, N. (1984). *Caring: A feminine approach to ethics and moral education.* Berkeley: University of California Press.

Rogers, M. B. (2000). *Barbara Jordan: American hero.* New York: Bantam Books.

Sherman, M. (Ed.). (2007). *Speaking the truth with eloquent thunder.* Austin, TX: University of Texas Press.

Siddle Walker, V., & Snarey, J. R. (2004). *Race-ing moral formation: African American perspectives on care and justice.* New York: Teachers College Press.

Smith, D. E. (1987). *The everyday world as problematic.* Boston: Northeastern University Press.

Spain, D. (1992). *Gendered spaces.* Chapel Hill, NC: University of North Carolina.

Stillman, R. J. (2006). Exploring films about ethical leadership: Can lessons be learned? *Public Administration and Management, 11*(3), 103-305.

Theoharis, G. (2007). Social justice educational leaders and resistance: Toward a theory of social justice leadership. *Educational Administration Quarterly, 43*(2), 221-258.

Tronto, J. (1987). Beyond gender difference to a theory of care. *Signs: Journal for Women and Culture in Society, 12,* 644-663.

Turner, C. S. V. (2002). Women of color in academe: Living with multiple marginality. *Journal of Higher Education, 17*(4), 355-370.

Warner, J. (2007). *The rhetoric of silence as a tool of empowerment in the life and works of Audre Lorde.* M.A. dissertation, Southern Connecticut State University, United States–Connecticut. Retrieved December 20, 2010, from Dissertations & Theses: A&I. (Publication No. AAT 1446328).

Zanetti, L. A. (2004). Repositioning the ethical imperative: Critical theory Recht, and tempered radicals in public service. *American Review of Public Administration, 34*(2), 134-150.

Video Resources: Teaching/learning tools to be used as supplementary material to support and expand the given topic.

- *A Litany for Survival: The Life of Audre Lorde* (1995) DVD
- *American Me* (1992) – featuring: Edward James Olmos, William Forsythe, Pepe Serna, and Evelina Fernandez
- *And the Band Played On* (1993) – featuring Alan Alda, Matthew Modine, and Lillie Tomlin
- *Barbara Jordan*–video clips *http://txtell.lib.utexas.edu/stories/media/j0001-video.html*
- *Barbara Jordan 1974 Nixon Impeachment:* *http://watergate.info/impeachment/74-0725_barbara-jordan.shtml*
- *Barbara Jordan 1976 Democratic Convention Keynote* *http://www.dailymotion.com/video/x6mh3i_barbara-jordan-s-1976-keynote-addre_news*

- *Cry Freedom* (1987) – featuring Denzel Washington and Kevin Kline
- *Ghandi* (1982) – featuring Ben Kingsley
- *Hotel Rwanda* (2005) – featuring Don Cheadle, Sophie Okonedo, Nick Nolte and Joaquin Phoenix
- *Hurricane* (1999) – featuring Denzel Washington, Vincent Pastore, and Don Hedaya
- *Lone Star* (1996) – featuring Matthew McConaughey and Chris Cooper
- *Rabbit Proof Fence* (2002) – featuring Kenneth Branagh, Everlyn Sampi, Tianna Sansbury, and Laura Monaghan
- *The Contender* (2000) – featuring Jeff Bridges, Gary Oldman, and Joan Allen
- *The Edge of Each Other's Battles: The Vision of Audre Lorde:* www.jenniferabod.com/audrelorde/index.htm
- *The Last of the Mohicans* (1992) – featuring Daniel Day Lewis, Madeline Stowe, and Jodhi May

References

Adler, S., Laney, J., & Packer, M. (1993). *Managing women: Feminism and power in educational management.* Philadelphia, PA: Open University Press.

Alston, J. A. (in press). An ethic of responsibility: A Black lesbian scholar ponders the intersection of racism and heterosexism in educational leadership. In R. Johnson & S. Jackson (Eds.). *The Black professoriat: Negotiating a habitable space.* New York: Peter Lang.

Anderson, V. (n.d.). The questions of ethics, indeed! Unpublished paper. Nashville, TN: Vanderbilt University.

Anderson, M. L., & Collins, P. H. (Eds.). (2009). *Race, class, and gender: An anthology.* New York: Wadsworth.

Andrews, W. L., Smith Foster, F., & Harris, T. (2001). *The concise Oxford companion to African American literature.* New York: Oxford University Press USA.

Beck, L. G. & Murphy, J. (1997). *Ethics in educational leadership programs: Emerging models.* Columbia, MO: The University Council for Educational Administration.

Beckner, W. (2003). *Ethics for educational leaders.* Boston: Allyn & Bacon.

Blackmore, J. (2002). Leadership for socially just schooling: More substance and less style in high risk, low trust times? *Journal of School Leadership, 12,* 198-222.

Bogotch, I. (2002). Educational leadership and social justice: Practice into theory. *Journal of School Leadership, 12,* 138-156.

Boxer, B. (1996, January 22). Life of Barbara Jordan. *Congressional Record Online.* Retrieved from http://www.elf.net/bjordan/boxer.html

Byrd, R. P. (2009). Create your own fire: Audre Lorde and the tradition of Black radical thought. In R. Byrd, J. B. Cole, & B. Guy-Sheftall (Eds.). *I am your sister: Collected and unpublished writings of Audre Lorde* (pp.3-36). New York: Oxford University Press.

Byrd, R., Cole, J. B., & Guy-Sheftall, B. (Eds.). (2009). *I am your sister: Collected and unpublished writings of Audre Lorde.* New York: Oxford University Press.

Cambron-McCabe, N., & McCarthy, M. M. (2005). Educating school leaders for social justice. *Educational Policy, 19*(1), 201-222.

Clines, F. X. (1996, January 18). Barbara Jordan Dies at 59; Her Voice Stirred the Nation. *New York Times.* Retrieved from http://www.nytimes.com

Collins, P. H. (1986). Learning from the outsider within. *Journal of Social Problems, 33*(6), S14-S32.

Collins, P. H. (1990). *Black feminist thought.* Cambridge, MA: Unwin Hyman.

Collins, P. H. (1998). *Fighting words: Black women and the search for justice.* Minneapolis: University of Minnesota Press.

Collins, P. H. (2000). *Black feminist thought: Knowledge, consciousness and the politics of empowerment* (2nd ed.). New York: Routledge.

Cornett, Z. J., & Thomas, J. W. (1995). Integrity as professionalism: Ethics and leadership in Practice. Retrieved from http://www.fs.fed.us/eco/eco-watch/ew960123.htm, October 29, 2010.

Crenshaw, K. (1989). Demarginalizing the intersection of race and sex: A Black feminist critique of antidiscrimination doctrine, feminist theory, and antiracist politics. *University of Chicago Legal Forum. 1989,* 139-167.

Crenshaw, K. W. (1991). Mapping the margins: Intersectionality, identity politics, and violence against women of color. *Stanford Law Review, 43,* 1241-99.

Dantley, M. (2002). Uprooting and replacing positivism, the melting pot, multiculturalism, and other impotent notions in education leadership through an African American perspective. *Education and Urban Society, 34,* 334-352.

Dantley, M. E., & Tillman, L. C. (2006). Social justice and moral transformative leadership. In C. Marshall and M. Oliva (Eds.), *Leadership for social justice: Making revolutions in education* (pp. 16-30). Boston: Pearson.

DeVeaux, A. (2004). *Warrior poet: A biography of Audre Lorde.* New York: W. W. Norton.

Du Bois, B. (1983). Passionate scholarship: Notes on values, knowing and method in feminist social science. In G. Bowles & R. D. Klein (Eds.), *Theories of women's studies* (pp. 105-116). London: Routledge.

Farnham, C. (Ed.). (1987). Gender differences in the perception of administrative role demands. Paper presented at the American Educational Research Association Annual Meeting. (ED 285 277).

Fletcher, J. (1966). *Situation ethics: The new morality.* Louisville, KY: Westminster John Knox Press.

Fulton, D. S. (2006). *Speaking power: Black feminist orality in women's narratives of slavery.* New York: SUNY.

Furman, G. C. (2003, Fall). Moral leadership and the ethic of community. *Values and Ethics in Educational Administration, 2*(1), 1-8.

Furman, G. C., & Gruenewald, D. A. (2004). Expanding the landscape of social justice: A critical ecological analysis. *Educational Administration Quarterly, 40,* 49-78.

Gates, H. L., & West, C. (2000). *The African American century: How Black Americans have shaped our country.* New York: Simon & Schuster.

Gilligan, C. (1982). *In a different voice.* Cambridge, MA: Harvard University Press.

Gilligan, C. (1993). *In a different voice.* (2nd Edition). Cambridge, MA: Harvard University Press.

Glazer, J. S. (1981). Feminism and professionalism in teaching and educational administration. *Educational Administration Quarterly, 27*(3), 321-342.

Gosetti, P. P., & Rusch, E. (1995). Reexamining educational leadership: Challenging assumptions. In D. Dunlap & P. Schmuck (Eds.). *Women leading in education* (pp. 11-35). New York: State University of New York Press.

Grady, S. (1996, January 23). Magnificent Voice Stilled at Last, *Philadelphia Daily News.* http://www.philly.com.

Gressgard, R. (2008). Mind the gap: Intersectionality, complexity, and 'the event'. *Theory and Science, 10*(1), 1-16.

Hammond, K. (1981). Audre Lorde: Interview. *Denver Quarterly, 16,* 10-27.

Harding, S. (1986). *The science question in feminism.* Ithaca, NY: Cornell University Press.

Harding, S. (1991). *Whose science? Whose knowledge? Thinking from women's lives.* Ithaca, N.Y.: Cornell University Press.

Hart, A. W. (1995). Women ascending to leadership: The organizational socialization of principals. In D. Dunlap & P. Schmuck (Eds.). *Women leading in education.* Albany, NY: State University of New York Press.

Holmes, B. A. (2000). *A private woman in public spaces: Barbara Jordan's speeches on ethics, public religion, and law.* Harrisburg, PA: Trinity Press International.

hooks, b. (1981). *Ain't I a woman: Black women and feminism.* Boston: South End Press.

hooks, b. (1984). *Feminist theory from margin to center.* Boston: South End Press.

hooks, b. (1989). *Talking back: Thinking feminist.* Boston: South End Press.

Jones, S. N. (2003). *The praxis of Black female educational leadership from a systems thinking perspective.* Unpublished Dissertation, Bowling Green State University, Bowling Green, OH.

Jordan, B. (1976, July 12). Democratic Convention Keynote Address: "Who will speak for the common good?" New York.

Jordan, B. (1992, July 13). Democratic Convention Keynote Address: "Change: From what to what?" New York.

Jordan, B. (1996). Ethic of responsibility. 27 *Tex. Tech L. Rev.* 1435

Jordan, B., & Hearon, S. (1979). *Barbara Jordan: A self-portrait.* New York: Doubleday.

Kezar, A. (2000). Pluralistic leadership: Incorporating diverse voices. *The Journal of Higher Education, 71*(6) 722-743.

Klein, R. D. (1983). How to do what we want to do: Thoughts about feminist methodology. In G. Bowles & R. D. Klein (Eds.), *Theories of women's studies* (pp. 88-104). London: Routledge.

Kohlberg, L. (1984). *Essays on moral development, Volume II, the psychology of moral development: The nature and validity of moral stages.* San Francisco: Harper & Row.

Larson, C. & Murtadha, K. (2002). Leadership for social justice. In J. Murphy (Ed.), *The educational leadership challenge: Redefining leadership for the 21st century* (pp. 134-161). Chicago: University of Chicago Press.

Lorde, A. (1978). *The Black unicorn: Poems.* New York: W. W. Norton.

Lorde, A. (1980). *The cancer journals.* San Francisco, CA: Spinsters Ink.

Lorde, A. (1983). There is no hierarchy of oppression. In *From homophobia and education.* New York: Council on Interracial Books for Children.

Lorde, A. (1984). *Sister outsider.* Trumansburg, NY: Crossing Press.

Lorde, A. (1988). *A burst of light.* Ithaca, NY: Firebrand.

Lorde, A. (1988). Scratching the surface: Some notes on barriers to women and loving. In *Sister outsider* (pp. 45-52). Berkeley, CA: Crossing Press.

Lorde, A. (2007). *Sister outsider.* Berkeley, CA: Crossing Press.

MacKinnon, D. (2000). Equity, leadership, and schooling. *Exceptionality Education Canada, 10*(1-2), 5-21.

Marshall, C. (2004a). Social justice challenges to educational administration: Introduction to a special issue. *Educational Administration Quarterly, 40,* 5-15.

Marshall, C. (Ed.). (2004b). Social justice challenges to educational administration [Special issue]. *Educational Administration Quarterly, 40*(1).

Meyerson, D. E. (2001). *Tempered radicals: How people use difference to inspire change at work.* Boston: Harvard Business School Press.

Meyerson, D. E., & Scully, M. (1995). Tempered radicalism and the politics of ambivalence and change. *Organizational Science, 6*(5), 585-600.

Ngunjiri, F. W. (2010). *Women's spiritual leadership in Africa: Tempered radicals and critical servant leaders.* New York: SUNY Press.

Northouse, P. G. (2007). *Leadership: Theory and practice* (4th Edition.). Thousand Oaks, CA: Sage.

Parker, P. S. (2005). *Race, gender, and leadership: Re-envisioning organizational leadership from the perspectives of African American women executives.* New Jersey: Lawrence Erlbaum.

Rapp, D. (2002). Social justice and the importance of rebellious imaginations. *Journal of School Leadership, 12*(3), 226-245.

Reinharz, S. (1992). *Feminist methods in social research.* New York: Oxford University Press.

Rogers, M. B. (2000). *Barbara Jordan: American hero.* New York: Bantam Books.

Rusher, A.W. (1996). *Black women administrators.* Lanham, MD: University Press of America.

Sherman, M. (Ed.). (2007). *Speaking the truth with eloquent thunder.* Austin, TX: University of Texas Press.

Shields, C. M. (2004). Dialogic leadership for social justice: Overcoming pathologies of silence. *Educational Administration Quarterly, 40,* 111-134.

Siddle Walker, V., & Snarey, J. (2004). *Race-ing moral formation: African American perspectives on care and justice.* New York: Teachers College Press.

Starr, B. E. (1999). Essays: The structure of Max Weber's ethic of responsibility. *Journal of Religious Ethics, 27*(3), 407-434.

Tharps, L. (September 2004). Speaking the truth. *Essence.* http://www.essence.com

Theoharis, G. (2007). Social justice educational leaders and resistance: Toward a theory of social justice leadership. *Educational Administration Quarterly, 43*(2), 221-258.

Tyson, C. (1998). Response to coloring epistemologies: Are our qualitative research epistemologies racially biased? *Educational Researcher, 27*(9), 21-22.

Walker, A. (1984). *In search of our mother's gardens.* New York: Mariner Books.

Lessons for the 21st Century: Six Voices Speak

Let us use with care those living messengers called words.
-W. Q. Judge

There is power in the spoken word. Spoken words are a powerful impetus to make change come about. Words influence our thinking and reinforce concepts within the psyche, wherein true learning can take place. In the context of this book, learning from the lessons of the lives of Black women activists demands hearing from them directly in their own words. These words are the strongest way to open the door to the lessons that can be learned and applied to 21st century leadership. We have identified the following topics from which to hear our foremothers speak:

- Leadership
- Social Justice
- Education
- Faith & Service

The Voice of Mary McLeod Bethune (1875–1955)

On Leadership

- Invest in the human soul. Who knows, it might be a diamond in the rough.
- If we have the courage and tenacity of our forebears, who stood firmly like a rock against the lash of slavery, we shall find a way to do for our day what they did for theirs.

- We have a power potential in our youth, and we must have the courage to change old ideas and practices so that we may direct their power toward good ends.
- We live in a world, which respects power above all things. Power, intelligently directed, can lead to more freedom.
- There is a place in God's sun for the youth farthest down who has the vision, the determination, and the courage to reach it.

On Social Justice

- If we accept and acquiesce in the face of discrimination, we accept the responsibility ourselves. We should therefore protest openly everything that smacks of discrimination and slander.
- If our people are to fight their way up out of bondage we must arm them with the sword and the shield and the buckler of pride.
- What does the Negro want? His answer is very simple. He wants only what all other Americans want. He wants opportunity to make real what the Declaration of Independence and the Constitution and the Bill of Rights say, what the Four Freedoms establish. While he knows these ideals are open to no man completely, he wants only his equal chance to obtain them.
- The drums of Africa still beat in my heart. They will not let me rest while there is a single Negro boy or girl without a chance to prove his worth.
- If we have the courage and tenacity of our forebears, who stood firmly like a rock against the lash of slavery, we shall find a way to do for our day what they did for theirs.

On Education

- From the first, I made my learning, what little it was, useful every way I could.
- Cease to be a drudge, seek to be an artist.

- There is a place in God's sun for the youth "farthest down" who has the vision, the determination, and the courage to reach it.
- The whole world opened to me when I learned to read.
- Knowledge is the prime need of the hour.

On Faith & Service

- Faith is the first factor in a life devoted to service. Without it, nothing is possible, with it nothing is impossible.
- I do feel, in my dreaming and yearnings, so undiscovered by those who are able to help me.
- I plunged into the job of creating something from nothing. ... Though I hadn't a penny left, I considered cash money as the smallest part of my resources. I had faith in a living God, faith in myself, and a desire to serve.
- I leave you love. I leave you hope. I leave you the challenge of developing confidence in one another. I leave you a thirst for education. I leave you a respect for the use of power. I leave you faith. I leave you racial dignity. I leave you also a desire to live harmoniously with your fellow man. I leave you finally a responsibility to our young people.
- As I give, I get.

Sources: Bethune, 1955; Hanson, 2003; McCluskey & Smith, 2001; Smith 2001

The Voice of Septima Poinsette Clark (1898–1987)

On Leadership

- I have a great belief in the fact that whenever there is chaos, it creates wonderful thinking. I consider chaos a gift.
- My participation in this fight was what might be described by some as my first radical job. I would call it my first effort

in social action challenging the status quo. I felt that in reality I was working for accomplishment of something that ultimately would be good for everyone.

- I don't think that in a community I need to go down to the city hall and talk; I train the people in that community to do their own talking.
- I was working for the accomplishment of something that would be good for everyone, and I worked not only with an easy conscience but with inspiration and enthusiasm.

On Social Justice

- My philosophy is such that I am not going to vote against the oppressed. I have been oppressed, and so I am always going to have a vote for the oppressed, regardless of whether that oppressed is Black or white or yellow or what. I have that feeling.
- I've never been a person to fight–My mind wasn't nonviolent. And I don't think that I've gotten to the place today where my mind is quite nonviolent because I still have feelings at times I'd like to do something violently to stop people.
- Once we recognize and admit that the mass of Black people live as unmistakably colonized victims (yet more courageously as more than victims) of white America, there is no escape from the knowledge that white America and its systems of domination are the enemy.
- The air has finally gotten to the place that we can breathe it together.
- I grew up with the idea that women didn't have a word to say. But later on, I found out that women had a lot to say, and what they had to say was really worthwhile.

On Education

- What we are working for is an educational program that has become a resource and rallying point for scores of brave southerners who are leading the fight for justice and better race relations in these crucial days.

- It would be better to use people from the community in which they lived who could just read well aloud and write legibly, rather than trying to use the others.
- We didn't need anyone with a high school education, nor did we need anyone with a college education. We just wanted to have a community person, so that the illiterates would feel comfortable.
- Education is my big priority right now. I want people to see children as human beings and not to think of the money that it costs nor to think of the amount of time that it will take, but to think of the lives that can be developed into Americans who will redeem the soul of America and will really make America a great country.

On Faith & Service

- I am one dedicated person working for freedom.
- In both Huntsville, AL and Savannah, GA all the people are strangers to me...they have to learn to trust me. More time must be spent with potential leaders....They have to learn to believe in me and not the adverse publicity they hear about me and Highlander.
- I don't consider myself a fighter. I'd prefer to be looked on as a worker, a woman who loves her fellow man, white and Negro alike...and is striving with her every energy, working not fighting in the true spirit of fellowship to lift him to a higher level of attainment and appreciation and enjoyment of life.
- I love people and want to help them, to understand them, feel with them, share their troubles as well as their joys, do all I can toward assisting them to the attainment of a happier and more worthwhile existence.
- Clark (1962) stated, "by teaching and helping others raise themselves to a better status in life...that [she] would not only be serving [her] state and nation...but all the people,

affluent and poor, white and Black...In lifting the lowly, we lift likewise the entire citizenship.

Sources: Brown, 1990; Baumgartner, 2005; Clark, 1962, 1986; Hall & Walker, 2010; Rouse, 2001

The Voice of Fannie Lou Hamer (1917–1977)

On Leadership

- Whether you have a Ph.D. or a no D, we're in this bag together. And whether you're from Morehouse or Nohouse, we're still in this bag together. Not to fight or try to liberate ourselves from the men–this is another trick to get us fighting among ourselves—but to work together with the Black man, then we will have a better chance to just act as human beings, and to be treated as human beings in our sick society.
- There is one thing you have got to learn about our movement. Three people are better than no people.
- We have to build our own power. We have to win every single political office we can, where we have a majority of Black people...The question for Black people is not, when is the white man going to give us our rights, or when is he going to give good education for our children, or when is he going to give us jobs–if the white man gives you anything-just remember when he gets ready he will take it right back. We have to take for ourselves.

On Social Justice

- To support whatever is right, and to bring in justice where we've had so much injustice.
- A house divided against itself cannot stand. America is divided against itself and without them considering us as human beings one day America will crumble! Because God

is not pleased! God is not pleased with all the murdering and all the brutality and all the killing for no reason at all. God is not pleased that the Negro children in the state of Mississippi are suffering from malnutrition. God is not pleased because we have to go raggedy and work from ten to eleven hours for three lousy dollars! And then how can they say that in ten years' time we will force every Negro out of the state of Mississippi. But I want these people to take a good look at themselves, and after they have sent the Chinese back to China, the Jews back to Jerusalem, and give the Indian their land back; they take the Mayflower back from where they came, the Negro will still be in Mississippi! We don't have anything to be ashamed of in Mississippi and actually we don't carry guns, because we don't have anything to hide.

- Nobody's free until everybody's free.
- With the people, for the people, by the people, I crack up when I hear it; I say, with the handful, for the handful, by the handful, 'cause that's what really happens.
- If the Freedom Democratic Party is not seated now, I question America. Is this America? The land of the free and the home of the brave? Where we have to sleep with our telephones off the hook, because our lives be threatened daily.

On Education

- You see in this struggle, some people say, well she don't talk too good. The type of education that we get here, years to come, you won't talk too good. The type of education that we get in the state of Mississippi will make our minds so narrow, it won't coordinate with our big bodies. We know we have a long fight, because our leaders, like the preachers and the teachers, they are failing to stand up today. But we know some of the reasons for that. This brainwashed education that the teachers have got.

- I may not have all the education but I do have common sense, and I know how to treat people.
- I am determined to become a first class citizen.

On Faith & Service

- You know I work for the liberation of all people, because when I liberate myself, I'm liberating other people.
- I have been tired for 46 years and my parents were tired before me and their parents were tired; and I have always wanted to do something that would help some of the things I would see going on among Negroes that I didn't like then and I don't like now.... All my life I've been sick and tired. Now I'm sick and tired of being sick and tired.

Sources: Hamlet, 1996; Jordan, 1972; Lee, 2000, 2001; Mills, 1993

The Voice of Shirley Chisholm (1924–2005)

On Leadership

- I am, was, and always will be a catalyst for change.
- No one has the right to call himself a leader unless he dares to lead.
- You don't make progress by standing on the sidelines, whimpering and complaining. You make progress by implementing ideas.
- Don't let your spirit die. We've learned a lot from our errors.
- I ran because someone had to do it first.

On Social Justice

- Laws will not eliminate prejudice from the hearts of human beings. But that is no reason to allow prejudice to continue to be enshrined in our laws to perpetuate injustice through inaction.

- Unless we start to fight and defeat the enemies in our own country, poverty and racism, and make our talk of equality and opportunity ring true, we are exposed in the eyes of the world as hypocrites when we talk about making people free.
- It is true that women are second-class citizens, just as Black people are. I want the time to come when we can be as blind to sex as we are to color.
- In the end anti-Black, anti-female, and all forms of discrimination are equivalent to the same thing—anti-humanism.
- I am not anti-white, because I understand that white people, like Black ones, are victims of a racist society. They are products of their time and place.
- My God, what do we want? What does any human being want? Take away an accident of pigmentation of a thin layer of our outer skin and there is no difference between me and anyone else. All we want is for that trivial difference to make no difference.
- Most Americans have never seen the ignorance, degradation, hunger, sickness, and futility in which many other Americans live. Until a problem reaches their doorsteps, they're not going to understand.
- Racism is so universal in this country, so widespread and deep-seated, that it is invisible because it is so normal.
- We Americans have the chance to become someday a nation in which all radical stocks and classes can exist in their own selfhoods, but meet on a basis of respect and equality and live together, socially, economically, and politically. We can become a dynamic equilibrium, a harmony of many different elements, in which the whole will be greater than all its parts and greater than any society the world has seen before. It can still happen.

On Education

- Women know, and so do many men, that two or three children who are wanted, prepared for, reared amid love and stability, and educated to the limit of their ability will mean more for the future of the Black and brown races from which they come than any number of neglected, hungry, ill-housed and ill-clothed youngsters. Pride in one's race, as will simple humanity, supports this view.
- I'm a teacher. At heart, I have always been a teacher.

On Faith & Service

- Service is the rent we pay for the privilege of living on this earth.
- ... Rhetoric never won a revolution yet.
- Scarcity of people in power who are sensitive to the needs, hopes, and aspirations of the various segments of our multi-faceted society. We have become too plastic; we have become too theoretical...We need individuals who are compassionate, concerned, committed.
- My day has come and gone. I continue to be a mentor. I am helping a number of younger Black men and women who are running for offices on the local level. I help to teach them how to prepare speeches.
- As a teacher, perhaps I could use the talents...which I felt were there to do something that would be of service to society—especially children.

Sources: Biales, 2007; Blair, 2008; Chisholm, 1970, 1972, 1973, 2010; Lynch 2004

The Voice of Audre Lorde (1934–1992)

On Leadership

- I am deliberate and afraid of nothing.

- When I dare to be powerful–to use my strength in the service of my vision, then it becomes less and less important whether I am afraid.
- When we create out of our experiences, as feminists of color, women of color, we have to develop those structures that will present and circulate our culture.
- If I cannot air this pain and alter it, I will surely die of it. That's the beginning of social protest.
- I became more courageous by doing the very things I needed to be courageous for–first, a little, and badly. Then, bit by bit, more and better. Being avidly-sometimes annoyingly–curious and persistent about discovering how others were doing what I wanted to do.

On Social Justice

- My response to racism is anger. I have lived with that anger, ignoring it, feeding upon it, learning to use it before it laid my visions to waste, for most of my life. Once I did it in silence, afraid of the weight. My fear of anger taught me nothing. Your fear of that anger will teach you nothing also.
- I write for those women who do not speak, for those who do not have a voice because they were so terrified, because we are taught to respect fear more than ourselves. We've been taught that silence would save us, but it won't.
- It is not our differences that divide us. It is our inability to recognize, accept, and celebrate those differences.
- We must be the change we wish to see in the world.
- There is no such thing as a single-issue struggle because we do not live single-issue lives.
- Battling racism and battling heterosexism and battling apartheid share the same urgency inside me as battling cancer.
- In our work and in our living, we must recognize that difference is a reason for celebration and growth, rather than a reason for destruction.

On Education

- The sharing of joy, whether physical, emotional, psychic, or intellectual, forms a bridge between the sharers which can be the basis for understanding much of what is not shared between them, and lessens the threat of their difference.
- There are no new ideas. There are only new ways of making them felt.
- The learning process is something you can incite, literally incite, like a riot.
- Our feelings are our most genuine paths to knowledge.

On Faith & Service

- Life is very short and what we have to do must be done in the now.
- The quality of light by which we scrutinize our lives has direct bearing upon the product which we live, and upon the changes which we hope to bring about through those lives.
- I feel a responsibility for myself, for those people who can now read and feel and need what I have to say, and for women and men who come after me. But primarily I think of my responsibility in terms of women because there are many voices for men. There are very few voices for women and particularly very few voices for Black women, speaking from the center of consciousness, for the *I am* out to the *we are*.

Sources: Byrd, Cole, & Guy-Sheftall, 2009; Lorde, 1978, 1980, 1983, 1984, 1988

The Voice of Barbara Jordan (1936-1996)

On Leadership

- The imperative is to find what is right and to do it.
- How do you judge if an action might be unethical?...Your entire life experience informs, nurtures, and tutors your ethical instincts.
- All I really need to know about how to live and what to do and how to be I learned in kindergarten. Wisdom was not at the top of the graduate [law] school mountain, but there in the sandbox at Sunday school. These are the things I learned: Share everything. Play fair. Don't hit people. Put things back where you found them. Clean up your own mess. Don't take things that aren't yours. Say you're sorry when you hurt somebody. Wash your hands before you eat. Flush. Warm cookies and cold milk are good for you. Live a balanced life–learn some and think some and draw and paint and sing and dance and play and work every day some. Take a nap every afternoon. When you go out into the world, watch out for traffic, hold hands, and stick together. Be aware of wonder. Remember the little seed in the styrofoam cup: The roots go down and the plant goes up and nobody really knows how or why, but we are all like that. Goldfish and hamsters and white mice and even the little seed in the styrofoam cup–they all die. So do we. And then remember the Dick-and-Jane books and the first word you learned-the biggest word of all–LOOK. Everything you need to know is in there somewhere. The Golden Rule and love and basic sanitation. Ecology and politics and equality and sane living. Think of what a better world it would be if we all–the whole world–had cookies and milk about three o'clock every afternoon and then lay down with our blankies for a nap. Or if all governments had as a basic policy to always put things back where we found them and to clean up their own mess. And it is still true, no matter how old

you are–when you go out into the world, it is best to hold hands and stick together.

- Vision is a requirement of leadership. Without it one becomes mired in the present with no clue about goals, ends, or future. A lack of vision gives support to whatever negatives this present moment embraces. If the society allows existing wrongs to go unchallenged, the impression is created that such wrongs have the support of the majority, and as a consequence, they sail unchallenged into the future.

On Social Justice

- As a nation with a long history of immigration and commitment to the rule of law, this country must set limits on who can enter and then credibly enforce our immigration law.
- The Commission decries hostility and discrimination against immigrants as antithetical to the traditions and interests of the country. At the same time, we disagree with those who would label efforts to control immigration as being inherently anti-immigrant. Rather, it is both a right and a responsibility of a democratic society to manage immigration so that it serves the national interest.
- Throw away your crutches and quit complaining because you are Black. Don't belch, choke, smoke, and wish for something to go away. Because when you are finished belching, choking, smoking, and wishing, society will still be here.

On Education

- Education remains the ticket to success in the majority community. Education is the ticket out–the ticket out of lives that have no hope of fulfilling their potential. Education is the ticket that will provide a Black student with the sense that he or she can make it in the world.

- No matter how well I prepared myself, society wasn't going to give me a chance to do much of anything else.
- Do not call for Black power or green power. Call for brain power.
- If you're going to play the game properly, you'd better know every rule.
- There is no obstacle in the path of young people who are poor or members of minority groups that hard work and preparation cannot cure.

On Faith & Service

- Give me a chance to show you.
- ...I am only fighting hard for things I strongly believe in.
- We are complex beings, and we seem to be bifurcated between an outer self and an inner self. In my opinion...the innate nature of man is good, basically good. For me, our inner self seem, to be in touch with God and communicating with Him regularly. This inner self is likable, caring, compassionate.
- I cannot live my life not loving the people who surround me and call myself a Christian.

Sources: Holmes, 2000; Jordan, 1992, 1994, 1996; Sherman, 2007

Points to Consider

1. What is the relevance of these words for today's 21ˢᵗ century organization in each area: Leadership, Social Justice, Education, and Faith & Service?
2. Identify one quotation that resonates with you. Prepare a 20 minute inspirational speech based on the quote to address a group that you are leading.

Suggested Readings

Allen-Taylor, J. D. (n.d.). Septima Clark: Teacher to a movement. Retrieved from http://www.safero.org/articles/septima.html

Barnett, B. M. (1993). Invisible southern Black women leaders in the civil rights movement: The triple constraints of gender, race, and class. *Gender & Society, 7*(2), 162-182.

Baumgartner, L. M. (2005). *Septima P. Clark: The contributions of a lifelong social justice adult educator.* Houle Scholars Monograph 5, Athens, GA.

Biales, B. (2007). Shirley Chisholm: A catalyst for change. In E. A. Gavin, A. Clamar, and M. A Siderits (Eds.). *Women of vision: Their psychology, circumstances, and success.* (pp. 245-258). New York: Springer Publishing

Blair, D. (2008). Shirley Anita St. Hill Chisholm, "For the Equal Rights Amendment" (10 August 1970). *Voices of Democracy, 3,* 50-62.

Brown, C. S. (Ed.). (1990). *Ready from within, a first person narrative: Septima Clark and the civil rights movement.* Trenton, NJ: Africa World Press, Inc.

Brown, T. L. (2008). "A new era in American politics": Shirley Chisholm and the discourse of identity. *Callaloo, 31*(4), 1013-1025.

Byrd, R., Cole, J. B., &. Guy-Sheftall, B. (Eds.). (2009). *I am your sister: Collected and unpublished writings of Audre Lorde.* New York: Oxford University Press.

Charron, K. M. (2009). *Freedom's teacher: The life of Septima Clark.* Chapel Hill, NC: The University of North Carolina Press.

Chinn, S. E. (2002). Feeling her way: Audre Lorde and the power of touch. *GLQ: A Journal of Lesbian and Gay Studies, 9*(1), 181-204.

Chisholm, S. (1970). *Unbought and unbossed.* Boston, MA: Houghton Mifflin.

Chisholm, S. (1972, January). *Speech to announce candidacy for the U. S. presidency* New York.

Chisholm, S. (1973). *The good fight.* New York: HarperCollins.

Chisholm, S. (2010). *Unbought and unbossed.* (Expanded 40ᵗʰ Anniversary Edition). Washington, DC: Take Riot Media.

Clark, S. P. (n.d.). Septima Clark Papers at Avery Institute. Retrieved from http://avery.cofc.edu/clarkpapers.htm

Clark, S. P. (1962). *Echo in my soul.* New York: E. P. Dutton & Co., Inc.

Clark, S. P. (1980). Citizenship and gospel. *Journal of Black Studies, 10*(4), 461-466.

Clark, S. P. (1986). *Ready from within: Septima Clark and the civil rights movement.* (Cynthia Stokes Brown, Ed.) Navarro, CA: Wild Tree Press.

Clark, S. P., & Twining, M. A. (1980). Voting does count: A brief excerpt from a fabulous decade. *Journal of Black Studies, 10*(4), 445-447.

Collier-Thomas, B., & Franklin, V. P. (Eds.), (2001). *Sisters in the struggle: African American women in the civil rights-black power movement.* New York: New York University Press.

DeVeaux, A. (2000). Searching for Audre Lorde. *Callaloo, 23*(1), 65-67.

DeVeaux, A. (2004). *Warrior poet: A biography of Audre Lorde.* New York: W. W. Norton.

Hall, J., & Walker, E. P. (2010). I train the people to do their own talking: Septima Clark and women in the civil rights movement. *Southern Cultures, 1*(1), 31-52.

Hamlet, J. D. (1996). Fannie Lou Hamer: The unquenchable spirit of the civil rights movement. *Journal of Black Studies, 26*(5), 560-576.

Hanson, J. A. (2003). *Mary McLeod Bethune and Black women's political activism.* Columbia, MO: University of Missouri Press.

Hu-DeHart, E. (2001). Writing and rewriting women of color. *Journal of Women's History, 13*(3), 224-233.

Jordan, B. (1981). Interview with Barbara Jordan. *Educational Evaluation and Policy Analysis, 3*(6), 79-82.

Jordan, B. (1992, July 13). Democratic Convention Keynote Address: "Change: From what to what?" New York.

Jordan, B. (1994). Listen to that still, small voice. *The New Texas Agenda: The Governor's Appointee Newsletter*

Jordan, B. (1996). Ethic of responsibility. 27 *Tex. Tech L. Rev.* 1435.

Jordan, J. (1972). *Fannie Lou Hamer.* New York: Thomas Y. Crowell Company.

Kwakye, C. J. (2007). Mary McLeod Bethune & Black women's political activism. *History of Education Quarterly, 47*(4), 514-518.

Lee, C. K. (2000). *For freedom's sake: The life of Fannie Lou Hamer.* Chicago: University of Illinois Press.

Lee, C. K. (2001). Anger, memory, and personal power: Fannie Lou Hamer and civil rights leadership. In B. Collier-Thomas & V. P. Franklin (Eds.), *Sisters in the struggle: African American women in the civil rights-black power movement* (pp. 139-170). New York: New York University Press.

Ling, P. J. & Montieth, S. (Eds.). (2004). *Gender and the Civil Rights Movement.* New Brunswick, NJ: Rutgers University Press..

Lorde, A. (1978). *The Black unicorn: Poems.* New York: W. W. Norton.

Lorde, A. (1980). *The cancer journals.* San Francisco, CA: Spinsters Ink.

Lorde, A. (1983). There is no hierarchy of oppression. In *From homophobia and education.* New York: Council on Interracial Books for Children.

Lorde, A. (1984). *Sister outsider.* Trumansburg, NY: Crossing Press.

Lorde, A. (1988). *A burst of light.* Ithaca, NY: Firebrand.

Lorde, A., & Rowell, C. H. (2000). Above the wind: An interview with Audre Lorde. *Callaloo, 23*(1), 52-63.

McCluskey, A. T. (1989). Mary McLeod Bethune and the education of Black girls. *Sex Roles, 21*(1-2), 113-126.

McCluskey, A. T., & Smith, E. M. (Eds.). (2001). *Mary McLeod Bethune: Building a better world essays and selected documents.* Indianapolis, IN: Indiana University Press.

McFadden, G. J. (1993). Septima P. Clark and the struggle for human rights. In V. L. Crawford, J. A. Rouse, and B. Woods (Eds.). *Women in the civil rights movement: Trailblazers and torchbearers 1941-1965* (pp. 85-97). Bloomington: Indiana University Press.

Mills, K. (1993). *This little light of mine: The life of Fannie Lou Hamer.* New York, New York: Penguin Books.

Miroff, B. (2007). Movement activists and partisan insurgents. *Studies in American Political Development, 21*(1), 92-109.

Morris, M. K. (2002). Audre Lorde: Textual authority and the embodied self. *Frontiers: A Journal of Women Studies, 23*(1), 168-188.

Olson, L. C. (2000). The personal, the political, and others: Audre Lorde denouncing "The Second Sex Conference." *Philosophy and Rhetoric, 33*(3), 259-285.

Rouse, J. A. (2001). "We seek to know...in order to speak the truth": Nurturing the seeds of discontent—Septima P. Clark and participatory leadership. In B. Collier-Thomas & V. P. Franklin (Eds.), *Sisters in the struggle: African American women in the civil rights–black power movement.* New York: New York University Press.

Sherman, M. (Ed.). (2007). *Speaking the truth with eloquent thunder.* Austin, TX: University of Texas Press.

Simien, E. M. (2003). Black leadership and civil rights: Transforming the curriculum, inspiring student activism. *Political Science and Politics, 36*(4), 747-750.

Smith, E. M. (2001). "Closed Doors": Mary McLeod Bethune on Civil Rights. In B. Collier-Thomas & V. P. Franklin (Eds.), *Sisters in the struggle: African American women in the civil rights–black power movement.* New York: New York University Press.

Video Resources: Teaching/learning tools to be used as supplementary material to support and expand the given topic.

- *A Litany for Survival: The Life of Audre Lorde* (1995) DVD
- *Barbara Jordan: http://txtell.lib.utexas.edu/stories/media/j0001-video.html*

- *Barbara Jordan http://watergate.info/impeachment/74-0725_barbara-jordan.shtml*
- *Barbara Jordan 1976 Democratic Convention Keynote http://www.dailymotion.com/video/x6mh3i_barbara-jordan-s-1976-keynote-addre_news*
- *Chisholm '72: Unbought and Unbossed* (2004)–PBS Video
- *Fannie Lou Hamer: Everyday Battle* (DVD, 2004)
- *Fannie Lou Hamer*–Testimony at the 1964 Democratic National Convention: http://www.zimbio.com/watch/xcXxe M0SJF/Fannie+Lou+Hamer+Testimony+1964+Democratic/ A+Celebration+of+Women%27s+History
- *Fannie Lou Hamer: Voting Rights Activists & Civil Rights Leader* (DVD, 2010); www.amazon.com
- *Mary McLeod Bethune: Champion for Education:* www.tmwmedia.com/Black_american_experience.html
- *Shirley Chisholm: First Black Congresswoman:* www.tmwmedia.com/Black_american_experience.html
- *The Edge of Each Other's Battles: The Vision of Audre Lorde:* http://www.jenniferabod.com/audrelorde/index.htm

References

Baumgartner, L. M. (2005). *Septima P. Clark: The contributions of a lifelong social justice adult educator.* Houle Scholars Monograph 5, Athens, GA.

Biales, B. (2007). Shirley Chisholm: A catalyst for change. In E. A. Gavin, A. Clamar, and M. A Siderits (Eds.). *Women of vision: Their psychology, circumstances, and success.* (pp. 245 - 258). New York: Springer Publishing.

Blair, D. (2008). Shirley Anita St. Hill Chisholm, "For the Equal Rights Amendment" (10 August 1970). *Voices of Democracy, 3,* 50-62.

Brown, C. S. (Ed.). (1990). *Ready from within, a first person narrative: Septima Clark and the civil rights movement.* Trenton, NJ: Africa World Press, Inc.

Byrd, R., Cole, J. B. &. Guy-Sheftall, B. (Eds.). (2009). *I am your sister: Collected and unpublished writings of Audre Lorde.* New York: Oxford University Press.

Charron, K. M. (2009). *Freedom's teacher: The life of Septima Clark.* Chapel Hill, NC: The University of North Carolina Press

Chisholm, S. (1970). *Unbought and unbossed.* Boston, MA: Houghton Mifflin.

Chisholm, S. (1972, January). *Speech to announce candidacy for the U. S. presidency.* New York.

Chisholm, S. (1973). *The good fight.* New York: HarperCollins.

Chisholm, S. (2010). *Unbought and unbossed.* (Expanded 40th Anniversary Edition). Washington, DC: Take Riot Media.

Clark, S. P. (1962). *Echo in my soul.* New York: E. P. Dutton & Co., Inc.

Clark, S. P. (1986). *Ready from within: Septima Clark and the civil rights movement.* (Cynthia Stokes Brown, Ed.). Navarro, CA: Wild Tree Press.

Clark, S. (n.d.). BrainyQuote.com. Retrieved October 30, 2010, http://www.brainyquote.com/quotes/authors/s/septima_clark.ht ml

Hall, J., & Walker, E. P. (2010). I train the people to do their own talking: Septima Clark and women in the Civil Rights Movement. *Southern Cultures, 1*(1), 31-52.

Hamlet, J. D. (1996). Fannie Lou Hamer The unquenchable spirit of the civil rights movement. *Journal of Black Studies, 26*(5), 560-576.

Hanson, J. A. (2003). *Mary McLeod Bethune and Black women's political activism.* Columbia, MO: University of Missouri Press.

Jordan, B. (1992, July 13). Democratic Convention Keynote Address: "Change: From what to what?" New York.

Jordan, B. (1994). Listen to that still, small voice. *The New Texas Agenda: The Governor's Appointee Newsletter*

Jordan, B. (1996). Ethic of responsibility. 27 *Tex. Tech L. Rev.* 1435.

Jordan, J. (1972). *Fannie Lou Hamer.* New York: Thomas Y. Crowell Company.

Judge, W. Q. (n.d.) Wisdom quotes. Retrieved on December 16, 2010, http://www.katinkahesselink.net/other/wqjwisdom.html

Lee, C. K. (2000). *For freedom's sake: The life of Fannie Lou Hamer.* Chicago: University of Illinois Press.

Lee, C. K. (2001). Anger, memory, and personal power: Fannie Lou Hamer and civil rights leadership. In B. Collier-Thomas & V. P. Franklin (Eds.), *Sisters in the struggle: African American women in the civil rights–Black power movement* (pp. 139-170). New York: New York University Press.

Lorde, A. (1978). *The black unicorn: Poems.* New York: W. W. Norton.

Lorde, A. (1980). *The cancer journals.* San Francisco: Spinsters Ink.

Lorde, A. (1983). There is no hierarchy of oppression. In *From homophobia and education.* New York: Council on Interracial Books for Children.

Lorde, A. (1984). *Sister outsider.* Trumansburg, NY: Crossing Press.

Lorde, A. (1988). *A burst of light.* Ithaca, NY: Firebrand.

Lynch, S. (Director and Producer). (2004). *Chisholm '72: Unbought and unbossed.* (Documentary). REALside Productions.

McCluskey, A., & Smith, E. (Eds.). (2001). *Mary McLeod Bethune: Building a better world essays and selected documents.* Indianapolis, IN: Indiana University Press.

Mills, K. (1993). *This little light of mine: The life of Fannie Lou Hamer.* New York, New York: Penguin Books.

Rouse, J. A. (2001). "We seek to know...in order to speak the truth": Nurturing the seeds of discontent–Septima P. Clark and participatory leadership. In B. Collier-Thomas & V. P. Franklin (Eds.), *Sisters in the struggle: African American women in the civil rights–black power movement.* New York: New York University Press.

Sherman, M. (Ed.). (2007). *Speaking the truth with eloquent thunder.* Austin, TX: University of Texas Press.

Smith, E. M. (2001). "Closed Doors": Mary McLeod Bethune on Civil Rights. In B. Collier-Thomas & V. P. Franklin (Eds.), *Sisters in the struggle: African American women in the civil rights–black power movement.* New York: New York University Press.

The_air_has_finally_gotten_to_the_place. (n.d.). *Columbia World of Quotations.* Retrieved October 29, 2010, from http://quotes.dictionary.com/The_air_has_finally_gotten_to_the _place

Afterword

Writing this book has been a journey of self-discovery and confirmation that all things work together for the goodness of others. Unlike Dr. Alston's research stream, my research stream has morphed into focusing on Black women's leadership. Originally as a graduate student, I sought to focus on Black men's leadership because I was trying to debunk the notion that I *had* to focus on Black women because I was one. In all honesty, as a young woman, I grappled with my identity as a Black woman because I felt that my black womanhood was in competition with black manhood and the men I had grown to love (i.e., my father, uncles, brother, and potential mate). However, during my data collection on Black men's leadership praxis and presenting this data at national educational conferences, I began to see that although there may be common experiences between Black women and men as raced individuals, we experience life differently due to our gendered identities as Black women and men. It became apparent to me that the systems of racism and sexism greatly affect my livelihood, my spiritual stamina, and my leadership praxis. Whereas men have access to male patriarchy, my access and the access of Black women is limited as was the access of the women profiled in this text. This does not say that my or other Black women's potential for leadership praxis is not great: I clearly and definitively state that in our leadership walk, we may have to take longer strides and be more creative in our approach. This ideal is confirmed as we review the leadership lives of Fannie Lou Hamer, Septima Poinsette Clark, Mary McLeod Bethune, Shirley Chisholm, Barbara Jordan, and Audre Lorde.

When Dr. Alston asked me to co-author this text with her, I was simultaneously anxious and joyfully overwhelmed. I have known Dr. A only for 8 years, but it seems like eternity. She is family and my "mom"; which is one of the reasons why I will never call her "Judy." I have the utmost respect for her, as she has been an influential force in teaching me as well as showing me the importance of being a Black woman scholar. She witnessed the experiences I had in the academy when my research was solely focused on Black men's leadership. She walked with me every step of the way and made sure I stayed the course. Today, I stand tall because I have had incredible mentors such as Dr. A and Dr. Cynthia Tyson and a cohort of academic sisters, the Scholarly Divas. I see the reflection of my Black womanhood in their lives as I see bits of pieces of me in the reflective leadership stories of the women in this text. In conjunction with Dr. A, I believe that everything happens for a reason. This book is no accident and my kinship with her is no accident either. The lives and legacy of Fannie Lou Hamer, Septima Poinsette Clark, Mary McLeod Bethune, Shirley Chisholm, Barbara Jordan, and Audre Lorde are profiled in hope that *you* will see bits and pieces of yourself in their struggle for equity and justice through their leadership praxis. It is my hope that this text serves as a guide to the greatness one person can achieve.

Patrice McClellan, Ed.D.
November 24, 2010

Index